Innovate to Dominate

Transform Your Business with Cutting-Edge Ideas and Strategies

MONICA BALL

The presentation of the information is without contract or any type of guarantee assurance. The trademarks that are used are without any consent, and the publication of the trademark is without permission or backing by the trademark owner. All trademarks and brands within this book are for clarifying purposes only and are the owned by the owners themselves, not affiliated with this document.

Table of Contents

Chapter 1

Introduction to Innovation

The Need for Innovation in Modern Business

Innovation has become the lifeblood of modern business, a critical driver that propels companies forward in an increasingly competitive and dynamic marketplace. Without innovation, businesses risk stagnation, losing their competitive edge, and ultimately fading into obsolescence. The need for innovation in modern business cannot be overstated, as it touches every aspect of operations, from product development and customer engagement to internal processes and corporate culture.

Companies that embrace innovation are better equipped to respond to market changes, seize new opportunities, and mitigate risks. This agility is particularly crucial in today's fast-paced environment, where technological advancements and consumer preferences evolve rapidly. Businesses must continuously adapt to remain relevant, and innovation is the key to this adaptability. Whether through incremental improvements or radical transformations, innovative practices enable businesses to stay ahead of the curve.

One of the primary drivers of innovation in modern business is the accelerating pace of technological change. Technology has revolutionized how companies operate, creating new avenues for growth and efficiency. For example, advancements in artificial intelligence, blockchain, and the Internet of Things (IoT) have opened up unprecedented possibilities for enhancing products, optimizing supply chains, and personalizing customer experiences. These technologies not only improve existing processes but also enable entirely new business models that were previously unimaginable.

Innovation is not limited to technology alone. It also encompasses new ways of thinking, novel business strategies, and creative problem-solving approaches. Companies that foster a culture of innovation encourage their employees to think outside the box, experiment with new ideas, and challenge the status quo. This culture often leads to the development of innovative products and services that differentiate a company from its competitors. For instance, companies like Apple and Tesla have built their reputations on their ability to consistently deliver groundbreaking products that redefine industry standards.

Moreover, innovation drives customer satisfaction and loyalty. In a world where consumers have endless choices, businesses must continuously innovate to meet and exceed customer expectations. This can be achieved through personalized experiences, improved product features, and seamless service delivery. Companies that prioritize innovation in their customer interactions often see higher levels of engagement and retention. For example, Amazon's relentless focus on customer-centric innovation has made it a leader in e-commerce, setting benchmarks for convenience and customer service that others strive to emulate.

Innovation also plays a crucial role in addressing global challenges and contributing to sustainable development. As businesses face increasing pressure to operate responsibly, innovative solutions are essential for reducing environmental impact, enhancing social welfare, and promoting economic growth. Companies that integrate sustainability into their innovation strategies can not only improve their reputations but also realize cost savings and open up new markets. For instance, the adoption of renewable energy technologies and sustainable supply chain practices demonstrates how innovation can drive both profitability and positive social impact.

However, fostering innovation is not without its challenges. It requires a supportive organizational structure, a willingness to invest in research and development, and a tolerance for risk and failure. Companies must create an environment where employees feel empowered to take risks and learn from their mistakes. This often involves flattening hierarchical structures, encouraging cross-functional collaboration, and providing the necessary resources and incentives for innovation to thrive.

Leadership plays a pivotal role in driving innovation. Visionary leaders who prioritize innovation set the tone for the entire organization, inspiring their teams to pursue bold ideas and embrace change. These leaders recognize that innovation is a continuous process, not a one-time effort, and they are committed to fostering a culture of curiosity and experimentation. By celebrating successes and learning from failures, they create a resilient organization that can navigate the complexities of the modern business landscape.

Investing in innovation also means committing to continuous learning and development. As the business environment evolves, companies must ensure that their employees have the skills and knowledge to leverage new technologies and methodologies. This can involve providing training programs, encouraging lifelong learning, and staying abreast of industry trends. Organizations that prioritize employee development are better positioned to innovate, as they can draw on a diverse pool of expertise and perspectives.

Collaboration is another critical component of successful innovation. In many cases, the most groundbreaking innovations result from partnerships between companies, research institutions, and other stakeholders. Collaborating with external partners can provide access to new ideas, technologies, and markets, enhancing a company's innovation capabilities. For example, pharmaceutical companies often collaborate with academic researchers to develop new drugs, combining their expertise to accelerate the pace of discovery and commercialization.

Innovation also necessitates a focus on data and analytics. In today's data-driven world, businesses have access to vast amounts of information that can inform decision-making and uncover new opportunities. By leveraging data analytics, companies can gain insights into customer behavior, market trends, and operational efficiencies, enabling them to innovate more effectively. For instance, retailers use data analytics to optimize inventory management, personalize marketing campaigns, and enhance the overall customer experience.

Finally, the need for innovation extends to all sectors and industries. Whether in manufacturing, healthcare, finance, or retail, the principles of innovation apply universally. Each industry presents unique challenges and opportunities for innovation, and companies that can navigate these complexities will be well-positioned for long-term success. For example, the healthcare industry has seen significant innovation in telemedicine, digital health records, and personalized medicine, transforming how care is delivered and improving patient outcomes.

In conclusion, innovation is an indispensable element of modern business, driving growth, competitiveness, and sustainability. Companies that prioritize innovation are better equipped to navigate the complexities of the contemporary market, respond to changing consumer demands, and contribute to global progress. By fostering a culture of innovation, investing in technology and talent, and embracing collaboration and data-driven insights, businesses can unlock new possibilities and achieve enduring success. The need for innovation is not a passing trend but a fundamental imperative that will continue to shape the future of business. As businesses recognize the critical importance of innovation, it is essential to understand the practical steps they can take to cultivate and sustain a culture of innovation within their organizations. These steps involve strategic planning, resource allocation, and a commitment to continuous improvement.

Key Concepts in Business Innovation

Business innovation encompasses a range of concepts and practices that enable companies to thrive in competitive and ever-changing markets. At its core, innovation involves the creation and implementation of new ideas, products, services, and processes that deliver value to customers and drive growth. Understanding the key concepts in business innovation is essential for any organization aiming to remain relevant and successful.

One of the foundational concepts in business innovation is the distinction between incremental and radical innovation. Incremental innovation refers to small, continuous improvements made to existing products, services, or processes. These improvements often enhance efficiency, reduce costs, or add minor features that increase customer satisfaction. For example, a smartphone manufacturer might release a new model with a better camera or longer battery life. Incremental innovations are typically less risky and easier to manage, as they build on existing capabilities and market knowledge.

In contrast, radical innovation involves significant breakthroughs that fundamentally change the way a product, service, or process operates. These innovations can create entirely new markets or disrupt existing ones. An example of radical innovation is the development of the electric car, which challenged the traditional automotive industry and set new standards for sustainability and efficiency. Radical innovations often require substantial investment in research and development and a willingness to take on higher levels of risk. However, they also have the potential to deliver substantial returns and secure a competitive advantage.

Another critical concept is the innovation funnel, which is a structured process for managing the flow of ideas from inception to implementation. The funnel typically involves several stages, including idea generation, screening, development, and commercialization. During the idea generation phase, companies encourage employees, customers, and other stakeholders to propose new concepts. These ideas are then screened to identify the most promising ones based on criteria such as feasibility, market potential, and alignment with strategic goals. The selected ideas move into the development phase, where they are refined and tested. Finally, the most viable innovations are commercialized and brought to market.

Open innovation is a concept that has gained significant traction in recent years. Unlike traditional innovation models that rely solely on internal resources, open innovation involves collaborating with external partners to co-create value. This approach recognizes that valuable ideas can come from outside the organization and that leveraging external expertise can enhance innovation capabilities. Open innovation can take various forms, including partnerships with startups, joint ventures with other companies, and crowdsourcing solutions from a broader community. By embracing open innovation, companies can access a wider pool of ideas, reduce development costs, and accelerate time-to-market.

Design thinking is another powerful concept in business innovation. It is a human-centered approach that emphasizes understanding the needs and experiences of end-users to create solutions that are both functional and desirable. The design thinking process typically involves five stages: empathize, define, ideate, prototype, and test. During the empathize stage, innovators immerse themselves in the user's environment to gain deep insights into their needs and challenges. The define stage involves synthesizing these insights to clearly articulate the problem to be solved. In the ideate stage, teams brainstorm a wide range of potential solutions. Prototyping involves creating tangible representations of the most promising ideas, which are then tested and refined based on user feedback. Design thinking fosters creativity and ensures that innovations are grounded in real user needs.

Disruptive innovation is a concept introduced by Clayton Christensen that describes how smaller companies with fewer resources can successfully challenge established incumbents. Disruptive innovations typically start in niche markets that are overlooked by larger competitors. These innovations may initially offer lower performance but provide unique benefits such as lower cost or greater convenience. Over time, they improve and move upmarket, eventually displacing established products or services. Examples of disruptive innovations include the rise of digital photography, which disrupted the traditional film industry, and streaming services like Netflix, which transformed the media and entertainment landscape.

The concept of a minimum viable product (MVP) is essential for rapid and cost-effective innovation. An MVP is a simplified version of a product that includes only the core features necessary to address the primary needs of early adopters. The goal of an MVP is to quickly validate assumptions, gather user feedback, and iterate based on real-world data. By launching an MVP, companies can test their ideas with minimal investment and reduce the risk of developing products that do not meet market needs. This iterative approach, often associated with lean startup methodology, allows for continuous learning and improvement.

Innovation ecosystems are another important concept. An innovation ecosystem is a network of interconnected organizations, individuals, and resources that collaborate to drive innovation. These ecosystems often include companies, universities, research institutions, government agencies, and other stakeholders. The synergy created by these collaborations can lead to accelerated innovation, as participants share knowledge, skills, and resources. Silicon Valley is a prime example of a thriving innovation ecosystem, where a dense concentration of tech companies, venture capital firms, and academic institutions creates a fertile ground for innovation.

The concept of frugal innovation, also known as Jugaad in India, emphasizes creating more value with fewer resources. Frugal innovation focuses on developing simple, cost-effective solutions that meet the needs of resource-constrained consumers. This approach is particularly relevant in emerging markets, where traditional innovation models may be too expensive or complex. Examples of frugal innovation include the development of low-cost medical devices, affordable housing solutions, and energy-efficient technologies. By adopting frugal innovation principles, companies can tap into new markets and address the needs of underserved populations.

Lastly, the concept of ambidexterity in innovation highlights the need for organizations to balance exploration and exploitation. Exploration involves seeking out new opportunities, experimenting with novel ideas, and taking risks. Exploitation, on the other hand, focuses on refining and optimizing existing capabilities to enhance efficiency and performance. Ambidextrous organizations are capable of simultaneously pursuing both exploration and exploitation, ensuring long-term sustainability and growth. Achieving ambidexterity often requires a dual structure, where different units or teams are dedicated to each approach, while leadership ensures alignment with overall strategic objectives.

Understanding these key concepts in business innovation provides a comprehensive framework for fostering creativity, driving growth, and maintaining a competitive edge. By distinguishing between incremental and radical innovation, managing the innovation funnel, embracing open innovation, applying design thinking, recognizing disruptive innovation, leveraging MVPs, cultivating innovation ecosystems, adopting frugal innovation, and achieving ambidexterity, companies can navigate the complexities of the modern business landscape. These concepts offer practical guidance for developing a robust innovation strategy that delivers sustained value and positions organizations for long-term success. In addition to understanding these foundational concepts, it is crucial for organizations to implement effective strategies and practices that bring these concepts to life. One such strategy is fostering an innovation-friendly culture within the organization. This involves creating an environment where creativity is encouraged, and employees feel empowered to take risks and experiment with new ideas. Leadership plays a pivotal role in shaping this culture by demonstrating a commitment to innovation and providing the necessary support and resources.

Historical Perspectives on Innovation

Innovation has always been the engine of human progress, driving civilizations forward through breakthroughs in technology, culture, and thought. Understanding the historical perspectives on innovation provides invaluable insights into how societies evolve, adapt, and thrive. This chapter delves into the significant epochs of innovation, illustrating how each era's unique circumstances and challenges spurred transformative advancements.

The ancient civilizations of Mesopotamia, Egypt, and the Indus Valley laid the groundwork for many of the innovations we take for granted today. In Mesopotamia, the invention of the wheel around 3500 BCE revolutionized transportation and trade. This seemingly simple innovation enabled the easier movement of goods and people, fostering economic and cultural exchanges that would shape the course of history. Similarly, the development of writing systems, such as cuneiform in Mesopotamia and hieroglyphics in Egypt, allowed for the recording and transmission of knowledge across generations, a foundational element for any advanced society.

The classical civilizations of Greece and Rome further expanded the horizons of innovation, particularly in the realms of philosophy, science, and engineering. Ancient Greek philosophers like Aristotle and Plato laid the intellectual groundwork for scientific inquiry and logical reasoning. Their emphasis on observation and experimentation would later influence the scientific revolution. Roman engineering feats, such as the construction of aqueducts and roads, demonstrated practical applications of innovative thought, enabling the expansion and maintenance of their vast empire. The Roman use of concrete, for example, allowed for the construction of durable and complex structures like the Pantheon, which still stands today as a testament to their engineering prowess.

The Middle Ages, often wrongly characterized as a period of stagnation, was actually a time of significant innovation, particularly in the Islamic world. Scholars in the Islamic Golden Age, such as Al-Khwarizmi, made groundbreaking contributions to mathematics that included the development of algebra. The translation movement in Baghdad's House of Wisdom preserved and expanded upon the knowledge of ancient civilizations, ensuring that crucial scientific and philosophical texts were available to future generations. In Europe, innovations in agriculture, such as the three-field system and the heavy plow, increased food production and supported population growth, laying the groundwork for the later economic expansion.

The Renaissance marked a pivotal moment in the history of innovation, characterized by a renewed interest in the classical knowledge of Greece and Rome and an explosion of creativity and intellectual activity. Figures like Leonardo da Vinci epitomized the Renaissance spirit of innovation, contributing to diverse fields such as anatomy, engineering, and art. The invention of the printing press by Johannes Gutenberg in the mid-15th century was arguably one of the most significant innovations of this period. It democratized knowledge, making books more accessible and affordable, and facilitated the spread of new ideas across Europe, which played a crucial role in the Reformation and the scientific revolution.

The scientific revolution of the 16th and 17th centuries was a period of profound transformation in the way humans understood the natural world. The works of Copernicus, Galileo, and Newton fundamentally changed the perception of the universe and laid the foundations for modern science. Galileo's use of the telescope to observe celestial bodies provided empirical evidence that challenged the geocentric model of the universe, while Newton's laws of motion and universal gravitation unified terrestrial and celestial mechanics under a single theoretical framework. These innovations not only advanced scientific knowledge but also demonstrated the power of systematic experimentation and observation.

The industrial revolution of the 18th and 19th centuries was another era of extraordinary innovation, fundamentally altering economies and societies. The development of the steam engine by James Watt and its application to machinery and transportation revolutionized industries and enabled unprecedented levels of production and efficiency. Innovations in textile manufacturing, such as the spinning jenny and the power loom, transformed the production process, leading to the establishment of factories and the rise of industrial cities. The industrial revolution also saw significant advancements in communication and transportation, with the invention of the telegraph and the expansion of the railway network, which connected distant regions and facilitated the movement of goods and people on an unprecedented scale.

The 20th century was marked by rapid technological advancements and the emergence of new fields of innovation. The invention of the airplane by the Wright brothers in 1903 opened up new possibilities for transportation and warfare. The development of the computer in the mid-20th century, with pioneers like Alan Turing and John von Neumann, laid the foundation for the digital age. The space race between the United States and the Soviet Union led to remarkable achievements, including the first human landing on the moon in 1969. These innovations not only pushed the boundaries of human capability but also had profound societal implications, shaping the modern world in countless ways.

The late 20th and early 21st centuries have been characterized by the digital revolution, driven by advancements in computing and telecommunications. The development of the internet transformed the way people communicate, access information, and conduct business. Innovations in mobile technology, such as the smartphone, have made information and communication tools ubiquitous. The rise of social media platforms has revolutionized social interactions and the dissemination of information, while advancements in biotechnology and renewable energy are addressing some of the most pressing challenges of our time, such as healthcare and climate change.

Throughout history, innovation has been driven by a combination of necessity, curiosity, and the desire to improve the human condition. The stories of individual inventors and thinkers, such as Thomas Edison, Marie Curie, and Nikola Tesla, highlight the importance of perseverance, creativity, and collaboration in the innovation process. Edison's development of the electric light bulb, Curie's pioneering research on radioactivity, and Tesla's contributions to alternating current electricity and wireless communication are just a few examples of how individual ingenuity has shaped the course of history.

Looking at historical perspectives on innovation, it becomes clear that each era's unique challenges and opportunities have shaped the trajectory of human progress. The interplay between societal needs, available technologies, and the individuals who dared to think differently has driven the continuous evolution of innovation. By examining these historical contexts, we can better understand the factors that foster innovation and apply these lessons to address contemporary challenges and seize future opportunities.

In summary, the history of innovation is a testament to human ingenuity and the relentless pursuit of improvement. From the wheel to the internet, each significant innovation has built upon the discoveries and inventions of previous generations, creating a cumulative legacy of progress. Understanding this historical journey enriches our appreciation of the present and inspires us to contribute to the ongoing story of human innovation. The history of innovation also highlights the importance of cultural and institutional support in fostering an environment where creativity can flourish. During the Renaissance, for instance, the patronage of wealthy individuals and families, such as the Medici in Florence, played a crucial role in supporting artists, scientists, and inventors. This financial backing provided the resources necessary for experimentation and exploration, leading to significant advancements in art, science, and technology.

The Innovation Mindset

Adopting an innovation mindset is crucial for anyone seeking to thrive in today's rapidly changing world. This mindset is not merely about generating new ideas but involves a holistic approach to thinking and acting that promotes continuous improvement and adaptation. It requires a blend of curiosity, resilience, and a willingness to take risks. To cultivate such a mindset, one must embrace certain core principles and practices that drive innovation both personally and professionally.

First and foremost, curiosity is the cornerstone of the innovation mindset. It fuels the desire to explore, learn, and understand the world in new ways. Cultivating curiosity means constantly asking questions and seeking answers, even in the face of uncertainty. It involves challenging the status quo and looking beyond the obvious. For example, consider the story of Steve Jobs and his fascination with calligraphy. His curiosity about typography and design ultimately influenced the development of the Macintosh computer, which set a new standard for user interfaces and aesthetics in personal computing.

Another critical element of the innovation mindset is the willingness to embrace failure as a learning opportunity. Failure is often stigmatized, but innovators understand that it is an inevitable part of the creative process. Thomas Edison's numerous attempts to create a workable light bulb are a classic example. Each failure provided valuable insights that eventually led to success. By reframing failure as feedback, innovators can iterate and improve their ideas, making each setback a step closer to achieving their goals.

Resilience, closely related to embracing failure, is essential for sustaining an innovation mindset. The path to innovation is rarely smooth, and setbacks are common. Resilience involves maintaining a positive attitude and perseverance in the face of challenges. It requires the ability to adapt to changing circumstances and to keep pushing forward despite obstacles. Innovators like Elon Musk exemplify this trait. His ventures, from SpaceX to Tesla, have faced numerous hurdles, yet his resilience has driven him to keep striving towards ambitious goals.

Collaboration is another vital aspect of the innovation mindset. Great ideas often emerge from the interplay of diverse perspectives and expertise. Building a network of collaborators who can offer different viewpoints and skills can significantly enhance the innovation process. For instance, the development of the polio vaccine by Jonas Salk was not a solo endeavor but a collaborative effort involving researchers, medical professionals, and volunteers. By fostering a culture of collaboration, innovators can leverage collective intelligence to overcome complex challenges.

Taking calculated risks is an inherent part of innovation. Innovators must be willing to step out of their comfort zones and venture into the unknown. This does not mean recklessly pursuing every idea but rather evaluating opportunities and making informed decisions about which risks to take. Jeff Bezos' decision to diversify Amazon from an online bookstore into a global e-commerce and technology giant involved significant risks. His strategic risk-taking has paid off, transforming Amazon into one of the most influential companies in the world.

An innovation mindset also involves a strong focus on customer needs and experiences. Innovators prioritize understanding their customers deeply and designing solutions that address their pain points. This customer-centric approach ensures that innovations are not only novel but also relevant and valuable. A prime example is the development of the iPhone by Apple. The company's relentless focus on user experience, from intuitive interfaces to seamless integration with other devices, revolutionized the smartphone industry and set new standards for consumer electronics.

Continuous learning is fundamental to maintaining an innovation mindset. The world is constantly evolving, and staying ahead requires a commitment to lifelong learning. Innovators seek out new knowledge, whether through formal education, self-study, or learning from others. They stay updated on trends, technologies, and best practices in their fields. Bill Gates, for instance, is known for his voracious reading habits and his constant quest for knowledge, which has helped him stay at the forefront of technological and philanthropic innovation.

Flexibility and adaptability are crucial for navigating the dynamic landscape of innovation. Innovators must be open to changing their approaches and pivoting when necessary. This flexibility allows them to respond to new information and emerging opportunities effectively. The story of Instagram's evolution from a location-based check-in app called Burbn to a photo-sharing platform highlights the importance of adaptability. The founders realized that users were primarily interested in the photo-sharing feature, prompting them to pivot and focus on that aspect, leading to Instagram's resounding success.

Empathy is another key component of the innovation mindset. Understanding and empathizing with the experiences and emotions of others can inspire more meaningful and impactful innovations. Empathy enables innovators to design solutions that truly resonate with users and address their needs. The design thinking methodology, popularized by IDEO, emphasizes empathy as a starting point for innovation. By deeply understanding users' experiences, designers can create products and services that provide genuine value and improve lives.

Effective communication is essential for conveying innovative ideas and inspiring others to support and adopt them. Innovators must be able to articulate their vision clearly and persuasively, whether to team members, stakeholders, or potential customers. Strong communication skills help build buy-in and foster enthusiasm for new initiatives. Steve Jobs' legendary keynote presentations, known for their clarity, passion, and storytelling, played a significant role in generating excitement and support for Apple's groundbreaking products.

An innovation mindset also requires a proactive approach to problem-solving. Innovators do not wait for problems to come to them; they actively seek out challenges and opportunities for improvement. This proactive stance involves anticipating future needs and trends and developing solutions before issues become critical. Henry Ford's development of the assembly line is a classic example of proactive problem-solving. By rethinking the manufacturing process, Ford was able to significantly reduce costs and production time, making automobiles more accessible to the general public.

Lastly, self-awareness and reflection are important for cultivating an innovation mindset. Innovators regularly assess their strengths, weaknesses, and areas for growth. This self-awareness enables them to leverage their strengths effectively and seek support or development in areas where they may need improvement. Regular reflection helps innovators stay aligned with their goals and adapt their strategies as needed. Journaling, seeking feedback, and setting aside time for contemplation are practical ways to enhance self-awareness and foster continuous improvement.

In summary, developing an innovation mindset involves embracing curiosity, resilience, collaboration, risk-taking, customer focus, continuous learning, flexibility, empathy, effective communication, proactive problem-solving, and self-awareness. By integrating these principles into their daily lives and work, individuals can unlock their creative potential and drive meaningful progress. The innovation mindset is not a destination but a journey, requiring ongoing effort and dedication. However, the rewards—both personal and societal—are well worth the investment. Through this mindset, we can not only achieve individual success but also contribute to a more innovative and prosperous world. To sustain an innovation mindset, it's essential to create an environment that nurtures creativity and encourages experimentation. This involves both physical and cultural elements. The physical workspace should be designed to inspire creativity, with open areas for collaboration, quiet zones for focused work, and spaces that stimulate thinking through visual and tactile elements. Companies like Google and Pixar are renowned for their innovative office designs that promote spontaneous interactions and creative thinking.

Overcoming Barriers to Innovation

Innovation is often touted as the lifeblood of progress, yet many organizations and individuals struggle to break through the barriers that stifle creative thinking and transformative change. Understanding and overcoming these obstacles is crucial for fostering an environment where innovation can thrive. From cultural resistance to organizational inertia, identifying the root causes of these barriers and implementing strategic solutions can lead to significant advancements and sustained growth.

One of the most pervasive barriers to innovation is fear of failure. This fear can be deeply ingrained in organizational culture, where the emphasis on success and perfectionism discourages risk-taking. Employees may hesitate to propose new ideas or experiment with unconventional solutions due to concerns about negative repercussions on their careers. To overcome this barrier, it is essential to cultivate a culture that views failure as a learning opportunity rather than a setback. Celebrating small wins and learning from unsuccessful attempts can encourage a more open and experimental mindset. Leaders should model this behavior by sharing their own experiences with failure and demonstrating resilience in the face of challenges.

Another significant barrier is the lack of resources, both in terms of time and funding. Innovation often requires dedicated time for brainstorming, research, and development, which can be difficult to allocate amidst the demands of daily operations. Similarly, securing funding for innovative projects can be challenging, especially in organizations with tight budgets or conservative financial strategies. To address this, organizations can set aside specific resources for innovation initiatives, such as dedicated time blocks for creative thinking, innovation labs, or small seed funds for promising projects. Encouraging cross-functional teams to collaborate can also maximize existing resources and foster a more integrated approach to innovation.

Organizational silos present another formidable barrier to innovation. When departments or teams operate in isolation, it hinders the flow of information and collaboration that are essential for generating novel ideas. This compartmentalization can lead to duplicated efforts, missed opportunities, and a lack of synergy. Breaking down these silos involves promoting a culture of collaboration and open communication. Regular inter-departmental meetings, collaborative platforms, and cross-functional projects can help bridge gaps and facilitate the exchange of ideas. Encouraging job rotation or temporary assignments in different departments can also provide employees with a broader perspective and foster a more cohesive organizational culture.

Resistance to change is a natural human tendency that can significantly impede innovation. This resistance can stem from a variety of sources, including comfort with the status quo, fear of the unknown, or concerns about increased workload and responsibilities. Overcoming this barrier requires effective change management strategies that address the emotional and practical aspects of change. Communicating the benefits and necessity of innovation, involving employees in the change process, and providing adequate training and support can help mitigate resistance. Highlighting success stories and quick wins can also build momentum and demonstrate the positive impact of innovative efforts.

Another barrier to innovation is the lack of a clear vision or strategy. Without a coherent direction, innovation efforts can become fragmented and aimless, leading to wasted resources and missed opportunities. A well-defined innovation strategy aligns with the organizational goals and provides a roadmap for identifying, prioritizing, and pursuing innovative ideas. This strategy should be communicated clearly to all employees, ensuring that everyone understands their role in the innovation process. Regularly reviewing and updating the strategy can also ensure that it remains relevant in a rapidly changing environment.

Inertia, or the tendency to maintain existing processes and systems, can also stifle innovation. This can be particularly challenging in well-established organizations with long-standing practices and bureaucratic structures. Overcoming inertia requires a deliberate effort to question and challenge existing assumptions and practices. Encouraging a mindset of continuous improvement and fostering a culture where questioning the status quo is valued can help break down this barrier. Implementing agile methodologies and iterative processes can also promote a more dynamic and responsive approach to innovation.

A lack of diversity can significantly hinder innovation. Homogeneous teams are more likely to think alike, limiting the range of perspectives and ideas. Embracing diversity in all its forms—cultural, gender, age, experience—can enhance creativity and lead to more robust solutions. Diverse teams bring different viewpoints and problem-solving approaches, which can spark new ideas and drive innovation. Organizations should actively seek to build diverse teams and create an inclusive environment where all voices are heard and valued.

Limited access to external knowledge and trends can also be a barrier to innovation. Organizations that are inward-looking and insular may miss out on valuable insights and opportunities from the broader market or industry. To overcome this, it is important to establish networks and partnerships that provide access to external knowledge and resources. Engaging with industry associations, attending conferences, and collaborating with academic institutions or other companies can help stay abreast of emerging trends and technologies. Encouraging employees to participate in external learning opportunities and bringing in external experts can also infuse fresh perspectives and ideas.

Finally, rigid organizational structures and processes can constrain innovation. Hierarchical decision-making, strict policies, and cumbersome procedures can slow down the innovation process and discourage initiative. To foster innovation, organizations need to adopt more flexible structures and agile processes. Empowering employees to make decisions, reducing bureaucratic red tape, and streamlining processes can create a more conducive environment for innovation. Encouraging a flatter organizational structure where information flows freely and decision-making is decentralized can also enhance agility and responsiveness.

In conclusion, overcoming barriers to innovation requires a multifaceted approach that addresses cultural, structural, and strategic factors. By fostering a culture that embraces failure, allocating resources for innovation, breaking down silos, managing change effectively, and developing a clear vision, organizations can create an environment where innovation can flourish. Embracing diversity, accessing external knowledge, and adopting flexible structures further enhance the capacity for innovation. These efforts collectively contribute to a more dynamic, creative, and resilient organization capable of navigating the complexities of the modern world and driving sustained growth and success. Building an innovative organization also requires an ongoing commitment to nurturing the right talent. Organizations should focus on attracting, developing, and retaining individuals who possess a creative mindset and a passion for innovation. This involves creating career development opportunities that allow for continuous learning and growth. Providing access to training programs, workshops, and mentorship can equip employees with the skills and knowledge needed to drive innovation. Additionally, recognizing and rewarding innovative contributions can motivate employees to consistently strive for creative solutions.

Chapter 2

Understanding Your Market

Analyzing Market Trends

Understanding market trends is crucial for any business looking to stay competitive and relevant. Market trends provide insights into the direction in which an industry is moving, the evolving needs and preferences of customers, and the strategies of competitors. By analyzing these trends, businesses can make informed decisions, anticipate changes, and seize new opportunities. This chapter delves into the methods and importance of analyzing market trends, offering practical advice for beginners to get started.

The first step in analyzing market trends is to gather relevant data. This involves looking at both quantitative and qualitative information. Quantitative data can include sales figures, market share, and financial performance, while qualitative data might involve customer feedback, expert opinions, and industry reports. One effective way to collect this data is through market research, which can be conducted using surveys, interviews, and focus groups. Additionally, secondary research sources such as industry publications, market analysis reports, and competitor websites can provide valuable information.

Once the data is collected, the next step is to identify patterns and trends. This requires a systematic approach to analyzing the data. Begin by categorizing the information into relevant segments, such as demographic groups, geographic regions, or product categories. Look for recurring themes and correlations within these segments. For example, a consistent increase in demand for eco-friendly products across multiple demographic groups might indicate a broader trend towards sustainability.

Technological advancements have made it easier to analyze vast amounts of data. Tools such as data analytics software and business intelligence platforms can help process and visualize data, making it easier to identify trends. These tools can highlight patterns that might not be immediately obvious, such as seasonal variations in sales or emerging market segments. By leveraging these technologies, businesses can gain deeper insights and make more accurate predictions.

Understanding the context behind the data is essential for accurate trend analysis. This involves considering the broader economic, social, and political environment. For instance, economic indicators such as GDP growth, employment rates, and consumer confidence can influence market trends. Social factors, including changing lifestyles, cultural shifts, and population demographics, also play a significant role. Political developments, such as new regulations or trade policies, can impact industries and market dynamics. By taking these contextual factors into account, businesses can better understand the drivers behind market trends.

In addition to quantitative analysis, qualitative insights are invaluable for understanding market trends. Engaging with customers directly through interviews, surveys, and focus groups can provide a deeper understanding of their needs, preferences, and pain points. Listening to customer feedback and observing their behavior can reveal emerging trends and unmet needs. Additionally, staying connected with industry experts and thought leaders through conferences, webinars, and networking events can provide fresh perspectives and insider knowledge.

Competitor analysis is another crucial aspect of market trend analysis. Monitoring the activities and strategies of competitors can provide insights into market dynamics and emerging trends. This involves tracking competitors' product launches, marketing campaigns, pricing strategies, and customer reviews. Understanding how competitors are responding to market changes can help businesses identify opportunities and threats. Additionally, benchmarking against competitors can reveal areas where a business can improve or differentiate itself.

To ensure a comprehensive analysis, it's important to adopt a forward-looking approach. While historical data is valuable for identifying past trends, predicting future trends requires a proactive mindset. This involves scenario planning and forecasting based on current data and trends. Businesses can use techniques such as trend extrapolation, regression analysis, and predictive modeling to anticipate future market developments. By considering multiple scenarios and potential outcomes, businesses can prepare for different possibilities and make strategic decisions with greater confidence.

Staying agile and adaptable is crucial in responding to market trends. The business landscape is constantly evolving, and trends can shift rapidly. Businesses need to be flexible and ready to pivot their strategies in response to new information. This requires a culture of continuous learning and innovation, where employees are encouraged to stay informed about industry developments and experiment with new ideas. By fostering an agile mindset, businesses can quickly adapt to changing market conditions and seize new opportunities.

Collaboration and knowledge sharing within the organization are key to effective market trend analysis. Cross-functional teams that bring together diverse perspectives and expertise can generate richer insights and more innovative solutions. Encouraging open communication and collaboration across departments can help break down silos and ensure that market insights are shared and acted upon. Additionally, creating a centralized repository for market research and trend analysis can ensure that valuable information is accessible to all relevant stakeholders.

Implementing a structured process for market trend analysis can help businesses stay organized and focused. This involves setting clear objectives, defining the scope of the analysis, and establishing timelines and milestones. Regularly reviewing and updating the analysis ensures that it remains relevant and aligned with business goals. Additionally, assigning responsibility for market trend analysis to specific individuals or teams can ensure accountability and consistency.

Finally, it's important to translate market insights into actionable strategies. This involves aligning business goals with market opportunities and developing a clear plan for implementation. For example, if the analysis reveals a growing trend towards online shopping, a business might invest in e-commerce capabilities and digital marketing. If customer feedback indicates a demand for more personalized products, a business might explore customization options or develop targeted marketing campaigns. By turning insights into action, businesses can stay ahead of the curve and drive growth.

In conclusion, analyzing market trends is a critical skill for any business looking to thrive in today's dynamic environment. By gathering and analyzing relevant data, understanding the broader context, engaging with customers, monitoring competitors, adopting a forward-looking approach, and staying agile, businesses can gain valuable insights into market dynamics. Collaboration, structured processes, and translating insights into actionable strategies further enhance the effectiveness of market trend analysis. With these practices, businesses can anticipate changes, seize new opportunities, and maintain a competitive edge in their industry. Consistency in conducting market trend analysis is key to staying informed and ahead of the competition. Regularly scheduled reviews—whether quarterly, semi-annually, or annually—can ensure that the organization remains updated with the latest market developments. Additionally, integrating this practice into the strategic planning process can help align the organization's long-term goals with emerging market trends.

Identifying Customer Needs and Pain Points

Understanding customer needs and pain points is the cornerstone of developing products and services that resonate with your target market. By identifying what your customers truly want and the challenges they face, you can create solutions that address these needs, leading to increased satisfaction and loyalty. This chapter explores practical methods and techniques for uncovering customer needs and pain points, providing actionable insights for beginners.

To begin with, listening to your customers is paramount. Engaging in direct conversations through interviews and surveys can reveal invaluable insights. When conducting interviews, ask open-ended questions that encourage customers to share their experiences and frustrations in detail. For example, instead of asking, "Do you like our product?" you might ask, "Can you describe a recent experience you had with our product?" This approach allows customers to provide more nuanced feedback, highlighting specific issues and unmet needs.

Surveys, on the other hand, can reach a larger audience and gather quantitative data. Designing effective surveys involves crafting questions that are clear and concise, avoiding leading questions that might bias the responses. Including a mix of multiple-choice questions and open-ended questions can provide both statistical data and qualitative insights. For instance, a question like, "What features do you find most valuable in our product?" followed by an open-ended prompt like, "Please share any additional feedback or suggestions," can yield comprehensive insights.

Observing customer behavior is another powerful method for identifying needs and pain points. By watching how customers interact with your product or service in real-time, you can gain a deeper understanding of their experiences and challenges. This can be done through usability testing sessions, where customers are asked to complete specific tasks while you observe and take notes. Pay attention to where they struggle, what confuses them, and what they find intuitive. These observations can reveal hidden pain points that customers might not articulate in interviews or surveys.

Analyzing customer support interactions can also provide valuable insights. Support tickets, chat logs, and call transcripts often contain direct expressions of customer frustrations and issues. By categorizing and analyzing these interactions, you can identify recurring problems and common pain points. For example, if multiple customers report difficulty in navigating your website, it may indicate a need for improved user interface design. Regularly reviewing and synthesizing customer support data ensures that you stay attuned to ongoing issues and emerging trends.

Social media platforms are another rich source of customer feedback. Monitoring mentions, comments, and reviews on social media can provide real-time insights into customer perceptions and experiences. Tools that aggregate and analyze social media data can help identify common themes and sentiments. Engaging with customers on these platforms by responding to their comments and questions can also build a deeper connection and show that you value their input.

Customer journey mapping is a strategic tool that helps visualize the entire experience a customer has with your product or service. By mapping out each touchpoint from initial awareness to post-purchase support, you can identify where customers encounter difficulties or drop off. This holistic view allows you to pinpoint specific stages in the journey that need improvement. For example, if customers frequently abandon their shopping carts during the checkout process, it might indicate a need for a more streamlined and user-friendly checkout experience.

Creating personas based on customer data can help in understanding the diverse needs and pain points of different segments of your market. Personas are fictional representations of your ideal customers, each with specific characteristics, needs, and challenges. By developing detailed personas, you can tailor your products, services, and marketing strategies to better meet the needs of each segment. For instance, a persona for a busy professional might highlight the need for convenience and efficiency, while a persona for a budget-conscious student might emphasize affordability and value.

Engaging with industry experts and thought leaders can also provide valuable perspectives on customer needs and pain points. Attending industry conferences, webinars, and workshops allows you to stay informed about emerging trends and best practices. Networking with other professionals and sharing experiences can uncover insights that you might not have considered. Additionally, reading industry publications and research reports can provide a broader context for understanding customer behavior and market dynamics.

Competitive analysis is another useful technique for identifying customer needs and pain points. By examining the strengths and weaknesses of your competitors, you can identify gaps in the market and opportunities for differentiation. This involves analyzing competitors' products, services, marketing strategies, and customer feedback. For example, if a competitor's product is highly praised for its ease of use but criticized for its lack of features, you might identify an opportunity to develop a product that combines both ease of use and robust functionality.

Innovative companies often go a step further by anticipating future customer needs and pain points. This involves staying ahead of industry trends and technological advancements, and continuously experimenting with new ideas. Encouraging a culture of innovation within your organization, where employees are empowered to explore and test new concepts, can lead to breakthrough solutions that address emerging needs. Regular brainstorming sessions, hackathons, and innovation labs can foster creativity and drive the development of cutting-edge products and services.

Feedback loops are essential for continuously identifying and addressing customer needs and pain points. Establishing mechanisms for regularly collecting and analyzing customer feedback ensures that you stay responsive to their evolving needs. This might involve setting up a dedicated feedback portal, conducting regular customer satisfaction surveys, and hosting customer advisory panels. By closing the feedback loop—acknowledging customer input, taking action, and communicating the changes made—you can build trust and demonstrate your commitment to customer-centricity.

Incorporating customer feedback into your product development and improvement processes is crucial for creating solutions that truly meet their needs. This iterative approach involves continuously refining and optimizing your products based on customer input. For example, agile development methodologies, which emphasize iterative development and frequent feedback, can ensure that customer needs are addressed throughout the product lifecycle. By involving customers in beta testing and pilot programs, you can gather real-world feedback and make necessary adjustments before a full-scale launch.

In conclusion, identifying customer needs and pain points is a multifaceted process that requires a combination of methods and techniques. By listening to customers through interviews and surveys, observing their behavior, analyzing support interactions, leveraging social media, mapping customer journeys, creating personas, engaging with industry experts, conducting competitive analysis, fostering innovation, establishing feedback loops, and incorporating feedback into development processes, businesses can gain a comprehensive understanding of their customers. This customer-centric approach enables organizations to develop products and services that not only meet but exceed customer expectations, driving satisfaction, loyalty, and long-term success. By integrating these practices into your organizational processes, you can create a culture that prioritizes and values customer insights. This culture shift is crucial for maintaining a competitive edge in today's rapidly evolving market. Let's explore how to embed these techniques into your company's DNA to ensure continuous improvement and alignment with customer needs.

Competitive Analysis Techniques

For any business looking to carve out a niche or dominate its market, understanding the competitive landscape is essential. Competitive analysis involves identifying your competitors, evaluating their strategies, and leveraging this information to inform your own business decisions. This chapter dives into practical and actionable techniques for conducting a thorough competitive analysis, providing beginners with a roadmap to gain a strategic advantage.

The first step in competitive analysis is identifying your competitors. This may seem straightforward, but it often requires a deeper dive than simply naming the obvious players. Start by categorizing your competitors into direct and indirect groups. Direct competitors offer similar products or services and target the same customer base. Indirect competitors, on the other hand, provide different products or services that satisfy the same customer need or solve the same problem.

Once you've identified your competitors, gather information on them. This can be done through various methods, including online research, customer feedback, and industry reports. Begin with their websites, which often provide a wealth of information about their product offerings, pricing, marketing strategies, and company values. Pay attention to their messaging and how they position themselves in the market. Tools like website analytics and traffic estimation platforms can give you an idea of their online presence and reach.

Social media is another valuable resource for competitive analysis. Analyze your competitors' social media profiles to see how they engage with their audience, the type of content they share, and the frequency of their posts. Social media listening tools can help track mentions of your competitors and gauge customer sentiment. This can reveal what customers like and dislike about their offerings, providing insights into potential gaps or opportunities in the market.

Customer reviews and testimonials are also crucial sources of information. Websites like Yelp, Google Reviews, and industry-specific review platforms can provide unfiltered feedback from customers. Look for recurring themes in the reviews, such as common complaints or praises. This can help you understand your competitors' strengths and weaknesses from the customer's perspective, which is invaluable when crafting your own strategies.

Industry reports and market research studies are excellent for gaining a broader understanding of the competitive landscape. These reports often include detailed analyses of market trends, industry growth projections, and competitive positioning. Subscribing to industry publications and joining professional associations can provide access to such reports. Additionally, attending industry conferences and networking events can offer firsthand insights from experts and peers.

Analyzing your competitors' marketing strategies is another key aspect of competitive analysis. This involves examining their advertising campaigns, content marketing efforts, and promotional activities. Look at their ad placements, the channels they use, and the messages they convey. Tools like SEMrush and Ahrefs can help you analyze their search engine marketing efforts, including the keywords they target and their backlink profiles. Understanding how your competitors attract and retain customers can inform your own marketing strategies and help you find ways to differentiate your brand.

Pricing analysis is a critical component of competitive analysis. Evaluate your competitors' pricing models to understand how they position their products or services in terms of value. This can involve looking at their pricing tiers, discount strategies, and any bundled offerings. Competitive pricing analysis can help you determine whether your pricing is competitive and identify opportunities for differentiation, whether through value-added features, superior customer service, or unique selling propositions.

Product analysis involves a detailed examination of your competitors' products or services. This includes evaluating their features, quality, design, and performance. If possible, try to experience their offerings firsthand by purchasing their products or using their services. This can provide insights into the user experience, the strengths and weaknesses of their products, and potential areas for innovation in your own offerings. Additionally, analyze how they handle product updates, customer support, and after-sales service.

Financial analysis can provide a deeper understanding of your competitors' business health and strategies. Publicly traded companies are required to disclose financial information, which can be accessed through their annual reports, SEC filings, and investor presentations. Key financial metrics to analyze include revenue growth, profit margins, and market share. This can help you gauge their financial stability and investment in growth initiatives. For privately held competitors, financial information might be harder to obtain, but industry reports and market analysis can provide estimates and insights.

SWOT analysis is a strategic tool that can synthesize the information gathered during your competitive analysis. SWOT stands for Strengths, Weaknesses, Opportunities, and Threats. By mapping out these four elements for your competitors, you can gain a comprehensive view of their competitive positioning. Strengths and weaknesses are internal factors, such as brand reputation, product quality, and operational efficiency. Opportunities and threats are external factors, such as market trends, regulatory changes, and emerging technologies. Conducting a SWOT analysis for your own business in parallel can highlight areas where you can capitalize on competitors' weaknesses or mitigate threats.

Benchmarking is another technique that involves comparing your business performance against industry standards or best practices. This can help identify areas where you lag behind your competitors and set improvement goals. Benchmarking can be done across various dimensions, such as customer satisfaction, operational efficiency, and innovation. Industry associations, research firms, and consulting companies often provide benchmarking data and services.

Scenario planning involves envisioning different future scenarios based on current trends and competitive dynamics. This technique can help you anticipate potential changes in the market and develop strategies to address them. For example, consider how your competitors might respond to a new market entrant, technological disruption, or changes in customer preferences. Scenario planning can help you prepare for various contingencies and stay agile in a competitive environment.

Regularly updating your competitive analysis is crucial for staying relevant and responsive. The competitive landscape is constantly evolving, with new entrants, changing customer preferences, and technological advancements. Establishing a routine for monitoring competitors and reviewing your analysis can ensure that you stay informed and proactive. This might involve setting up alerts for news about your competitors, subscribing to industry newsletters, and maintaining a competitive intelligence database.

Incorporating competitive analysis into your business strategy can lead to more informed decision-making and a stronger competitive position. By understanding your competitors' strengths and weaknesses, you can identify opportunities for differentiation, anticipate market trends, and develop strategies that leverage your unique advantages. This proactive approach can help you stay ahead of the competition and build a sustainable competitive edge.

In conclusion, competitive analysis is a multifaceted process that involves identifying competitors, gathering information, analyzing strategies, and continuously monitoring the competitive landscape. By employing techniques such as online research, social media analysis, customer reviews, industry reports, marketing analysis, pricing analysis, product analysis, financial analysis, SWOT analysis, benchmarking, and scenario planning, businesses can gain a comprehensive understanding of their competitors and the market. This knowledge enables businesses to make informed decisions, capitalize on opportunities, and mitigate risks, ultimately driving success and growth. Effective competitive analysis goes beyond just gathering data; it's about translating that data into actionable insights and strategic decisions. Here's how to put the insights from your competitive analysis into practice.

Leveraging Data for Market Insights

The modern business landscape is awash with data. From customer behavior to sales trends, from website analytics to social media interactions, data is generated at an unprecedented rate. For businesses, the challenge and opportunity lie in transforming this raw data into actionable market insights. Leveraging data effectively can provide a clearer understanding of market dynamics, customer needs, and competitive positioning, driving smarter decisions and strategic growth.

The journey to leveraging data for market insights begins with data collection. Businesses must identify the sources of data that are most relevant to their operations. Common sources include customer databases, sales records, website analytics, social media platforms, and market research reports. Each source offers unique perspectives and, when combined, can create a comprehensive view of the market.

Collecting data is just the first step. The real value lies in processing and analyzing this data to extract meaningful insights. Data analysis can take various forms, from simple descriptive statistics to complex predictive modeling. Descriptive analytics helps you understand what has happened in the past by summarizing historical data. For example, analyzing past sales data can reveal seasonal trends and peak purchasing times.

However, to gain deeper insights, businesses often turn to diagnostic and predictive analytics. Diagnostic analytics explores the reasons behind past outcomes. For instance, if there was a sudden spike in sales, diagnostic analytics can help determine whether it was due to a successful marketing campaign, a new product launch, or external factors like an economic boom. Predictive analytics, on the other hand, uses historical data to forecast future trends. By identifying patterns and correlations, predictive models can help businesses anticipate customer behavior, market demand, and potential risks.

To make data analysis more manageable and insightful, businesses often employ data visualization techniques. Visual tools such as charts, graphs, and dashboards transform complex data sets into intuitive, easily digestible formats. This not only aids in understanding the data but also in communicating findings to stakeholders who may not have a technical background. A well-designed dashboard, for example, can provide an at-a-glance overview of key performance indicators (KPIs), helping decision-makers quickly grasp the current state of the business and the market.

Segmenting your data is another powerful technique for deriving market insights. By dividing your data into meaningful categories, such as customer demographics, purchasing behavior, or geographic regions, you can uncover patterns and trends that might be obscured in aggregated data. Customer segmentation is particularly valuable, as it allows businesses to tailor their marketing strategies to different customer groups. For example, a company might find that younger customers respond better to social media marketing, while older customers prefer email campaigns. Understanding these preferences enables more effective and targeted marketing efforts.

Another critical aspect of leveraging data for market insights is benchmarking. This involves comparing your business's performance against industry standards or competitors. Benchmarking helps identify areas where your business excels and areas needing improvement. For instance, if your customer satisfaction scores are lower than the industry average, it may indicate that you need to enhance your customer service or product quality. Regular benchmarking ensures that your business remains competitive and can adapt to changing market conditions.

Businesses must also pay attention to external data sources, such as industry reports, market research studies, and economic indicators. These sources provide valuable context and can help validate internal data findings. For instance, if your internal sales data shows a declining trend, industry reports might reveal whether this is a market-wide issue or specific to your business. Additionally, staying informed about broader economic trends enables better anticipation of market shifts and strategic planning.

While the technical aspects of data analysis are important, the human element should not be overlooked. Data-driven decision-making requires a culture that values and understands data. This involves training employees to be data literate, encouraging curiosity, and promoting an analytical mindset. When employees at all levels are comfortable working with data, they are more likely to recognize valuable insights and apply them to their daily tasks.

Moreover, collaboration between departments enhances the quality and impact of data insights. Marketing, sales, finance, and operations teams often hold different pieces of the data puzzle. By sharing insights and working together, these teams can create a more holistic view of the business and market. For example, marketing insights into customer preferences can inform product development, while sales data can highlight successful marketing campaigns. Cross-departmental collaboration ensures that data-driven strategies are aligned and cohesive.

Data privacy and security are also paramount when leveraging data for market insights. Businesses must comply with data protection regulations, such as the General Data Protection Regulation (GDPR) in Europe or the California Consumer Privacy Act (CCPA) in the United States. Ensuring that customer data is collected, stored, and processed securely protects against data breaches and maintains customer trust. Transparency about data usage and obtaining customer consent are essential practices in today's data-driven world.

Finally, the effectiveness of leveraging data for market insights depends on continuous improvement. The market environment is dynamic, and what worked yesterday may not work tomorrow. Regularly reviewing and refining your data collection methods, analysis techniques, and strategies ensures that your business stays agile and responsive. Implementing feedback loops, where insights lead to actions, and actions are evaluated for outcomes, creates a cycle of perpetual learning and improvement.

In summary, leveraging data for market insights is a multifaceted process that involves collecting, analyzing, visualizing, and acting on data. By employing techniques such as data segmentation, benchmarking, and predictive analytics, businesses can gain a deeper understanding of market dynamics and customer behavior. Cultivating a data-driven culture, ensuring data privacy, and fostering collaboration across departments further enhance the ability to derive actionable insights. As the market continues to evolve, so must the strategies and tools used to harness the power of data, ensuring that businesses remain competitive and poised for growth? To truly maximize the benefits of leveraging data for market insights, businesses must also invest in the right tools and technologies. Advanced analytics platforms, customer relationship management (CRM) systems, and business intelligence (BI) tools can streamline data processing and provide more sophisticated analytical capabilities. These technologies enable businesses to handle large volumes of data efficiently and derive deeper insights through machine learning algorithms, real-time analytics, and predictive modeling.

Case Studies of Market-Driven Innovation

Innovation is often heralded as the lifeblood of business growth and sustainability. However, the most successful innovations are not merely the product of creative brainstorming or technological advancements; they are driven by a deep understanding of market needs and consumer behavior. By examining case studies of market-driven innovation, we can uncover valuable lessons on how to align innovation strategies with real-world demands and opportunities.

One of the most compelling examples is the story of Netflix. Founded in 1997 as a DVD rental service,

Netflix initially struggled to differentiate itself in a crowded market dominated by Blockbuster. The turning point came when Netflix leveraged data to understand customer preferences. By tracking rental patterns, they discovered that customers valued convenience and a wide selection of movies. This insight led to the creation of a subscription-based model with no late fees, a stark contrast to Blockbuster's penalizing system. Netflix's focus on customer convenience and choice was a game-changer, but their market-driven innovation didn't stop there.

As internet speeds increased and streaming technology improved, Netflix recognized a shift in consumer behavior towards digital content consumption. Anticipating this trend, they invested heavily in streaming technology, launching their streaming service in 2007. This strategic pivot not only met the emerging demand for online content but also positioned Netflix as a pioneer in the industry. Today, Netflix continues to innovate by using data analytics to inform content creation, ensuring that their original shows and movies resonate with audience preferences.

Another notable case is the transformation of LEGO. In the early 2000s, LEGO faced significant financial difficulties, with declining sales and increasing competition from digital entertainment. To revive the brand, LEGO embarked on a journey to reconnect with its core audience – children and their parents. The company conducted extensive market research, including ethnographic studies where designers spent time with children to observe their play habits. This research revealed that children were increasingly interested in storytelling and customization in their play.

Armed with these insights, LEGO introduced new product lines like LEGO Ninjago and LEGO Friends, which combined traditional brick-building with rich narratives and character development. These themes were supported by animated TV shows and interactive online content, creating an immersive experience that appealed to children's evolving interests. The success of these market-driven innovations reinvigorated LEGO's brand and led to a period of sustained growth and profitability.

Apple's journey with the iPhone is another exemplary case of market-driven innovation. Before the iPhone's launch in 2007, the smartphone market was dominated by devices with physical keyboards and limited internet capabilities. Apple's extensive market research indicated that consumers desired a more intuitive and versatile device that combined communication, entertainment, and productivity in a single platform. By focusing on user experience, Apple designed the iPhone with a touch-screen interface, a robust operating system, and access to a wide range of applications.

The introduction of the App Store in 2008 further demonstrated Apple's commitment to market-driven innovation. Recognizing the potential for third-party developers to create diverse applications, Apple opened its platform, allowing developers to contribute to the ecosystem. This move not only expanded the functionality of the iPhone but also fostered a community of innovation that continues to thrive today. The iPhone's success can be attributed to Apple's ability to anticipate and address consumer needs, setting a new standard in the mobile industry.

In the realm of food and beverage, the story of Beyond Meat illustrates how understanding market trends can lead to groundbreaking innovation. Founded in 2009, Beyond Meat aimed to address the growing consumer demand for plant-based protein alternatives due to health, environmental, and ethical concerns. Through extensive research and development, the company created a plant-based burger that closely mimicked the taste and texture of beef.

Beyond Meat's market-driven approach involved not only perfecting the product but also strategically positioning it in the market. They targeted meat-eaters and flexitarians rather than just vegetarians and vegans, emphasizing the environmental benefits and health advantages of their products without compromising on taste. By aligning their innovation with consumer values and dietary trends, Beyond Meat successfully entered mainstream markets, including partnerships with major fast-food chains and retailers.

Another instructive case is that of Tesla and its impact on the automotive industry. Tesla's founder, Elon Musk, identified a growing concern over fossil fuel dependence and environmental sustainability. Traditional automakers were slow to innovate in the electric vehicle (EV) space, often producing models with limited range and performance. Tesla's market-driven innovation focused on creating high-performance electric cars that appealed to both eco-conscious consumers and car enthusiasts.

Tesla's Model S, launched in 2012, was a game-changer. It offered a long driving range, impressive acceleration, and advanced technology features such as over-the-air software updates and autopilot capabilities. By addressing the key pain points associated with electric vehicles – range anxiety and performance limitations – Tesla redefined consumer expectations and accelerated the adoption of EVs. The company's continuous focus on innovation, such as developing more affordable models and investing in a global charging infrastructure, demonstrates their commitment to meeting market demands.

The case of Airbnb showcases how market-driven innovation can disrupt traditional industries. Founded in 2008, Airbnb emerged from the founders' personal experience of renting out an air mattress in their apartment to cover rent costs. They realized that there was a significant market for affordable and unique lodging options. By creating a platform that connected homeowners with travelers, Airbnb tapped into the growing trend of the sharing economy.

Airbnb's success can be attributed to their deep understanding of both hosts and guests. They developed features that addressed the concerns of both parties, such as secure payment systems, user reviews, and insurance coverage. Additionally, Airbnb continuously gathered feedback and analyzed usage data to improve their platform and expand their offerings. This market-driven approach enabled Airbnb to grow rapidly and challenge the dominance of traditional hotel chains.

These case studies illustrate that market-driven innovation is not about following trends blindly but about deeply understanding and anticipating consumer needs. Successful companies listen to their customers, analyze market data, and adapt their strategies to align with evolving preferences and behaviors. They invest in research and development, not just to create new products, but to ensure those products resonate with their target audience.

Moreover, market-driven innovation requires a willingness to pivot and take risks. Companies must be agile and ready to change course based on market feedback. This agility is evident in the stories of Netflix's transition from DVDs to streaming, LEGO's shift to narrative-driven playsets, and Tesla's focus on making electric vehicles desirable.

In conclusion, the power of market-driven innovation lies in its ability to create products and services that not only meet existing demands but also anticipate future needs. By staying attuned to market signals and maintaining a customer-centric approach, businesses can drive innovation that leads to sustained competitive advantage and growth. These case studies serve as a testament to the transformative potential of aligning innovation efforts with market insights, highlighting the importance of being responsive, adaptable, and deeply connected to the consumer landscape. Market-driven innovation is not just a strategy but a mindset that permeates successful organizations. This approach necessitates a culture where listening to the customer is paramount, and data-driven decision-making is embedded in every level of the organization. As we delve deeper into the mechanics of market-driven innovation, it becomes clear that certain principles and practices are consistently employed by companies that excel in this domain.

Chapter 3

Building an Innovative Culture

Fostering a Culture of Creativity

Creativity is often considered the cornerstone of innovation, and fostering a culture that nurtures creative thinking can significantly enhance an organization's ability to adapt and thrive. Cultivating such a culture requires a deliberate effort to create an environment where new ideas are welcomed, experimentation is encouraged, and employees feel empowered to express their unique perspectives. This chapter delves into various strategies and practices that can help organizations foster a culture of creativity, ensuring they remain competitive and relevant in an ever-evolving market.

One of the most crucial elements in fostering a culture of creativity is leadership. Leaders play a pivotal role in setting the tone for creativity within an organization. They must not only champion creativity but also embody it in their actions and decisions. This involves being open to new ideas, encouraging risk-taking, and being willing to challenge the status quo. Leaders should also be approachable and accessible, creating an atmosphere where employees feel comfortable sharing their thoughts and ideas without fear of judgment or retribution.

Creating a physical environment that inspires creativity is another important factor. The layout and design of the workplace can significantly impact the flow of ideas and collaboration. Open spaces that facilitate communication, areas designed for brainstorming, and quiet zones for focused work can all contribute to a more creative atmosphere. Incorporating elements such as natural light, plants, and artwork can also enhance the overall ambiance and stimulate creative thinking. By thoughtfully designing the workspace, organizations can create an environment that nurtures creativity and innovation.

Encouraging diversity within the organization is essential for fostering creativity. A diverse workforce brings together individuals with different backgrounds, experiences, and perspectives, which can lead to more innovative solutions and ideas. Diversity should be embraced not only in terms of race, gender, and ethnicity but also in terms of skills, experiences, and ways of thinking. By creating a diverse and inclusive environment, organizations can tap into a broader range of ideas and approaches, ultimately driving more creative outcomes.

Providing opportunities for continuous learning and development is another key aspect of fostering a culture of creativity. Encouraging employees to pursue new skills and knowledge can help them think more creatively and approach problems from different angles. This can be achieved through various means, such as offering training programs, workshops, and conferences, as well as providing access to online courses and resources. By investing in their employees' growth and development, organizations can cultivate a more creative and innovative workforce.

Recognizing and rewarding creativity is crucial for sustaining a culture of innovation. When employees see that their creative efforts are valued and appreciated, they are more likely to continue contributing new ideas and solutions. This recognition can take many forms, from formal awards and bonuses to informal acknowledgments and praise. Additionally, creating opportunities for employees to share their successes and learn from each other can help reinforce the importance of creativity within the organization.

A culture of creativity also thrives on collaboration and teamwork. Encouraging employees to work together on projects and initiatives can lead to the cross-pollination of ideas and the development of more innovative solutions. This can be facilitated through regular team meetings, brainstorming sessions, and collaborative platforms that enable employees to share their ideas and work together more effectively. By fostering a collaborative environment, organizations can harness the collective creativity of their workforce.

Encouraging risk-taking and embracing failure as a learning opportunity is another vital component of a creative culture. Employees need to feel that they can experiment and take risks without fear of negative consequences. This involves creating a safe environment where failure is seen as a natural part of the innovation process and an opportunity to learn and improve. Leaders should model this behavior by sharing their own experiences with failure and demonstrating how they have learned and grown from those experiences. By normalizing risk-taking and learning from failure, organizations can foster a more resilient and creative workforce.

Empowering employees with autonomy and ownership over their work can also enhance creativity. When employees have the freedom to make decisions and take initiative, they are more likely to explore new ideas and approaches. This empowerment can be achieved by providing clear goals and expectations while allowing employees the flexibility to determine how they achieve those goals. By giving employees a sense of ownership and control over their work, organizations can foster a more engaged and creative workforce.

Encouraging cross-disciplinary collaboration can also drive creativity. When individuals from different departments and areas of expertise come together to solve problems, they can bring unique perspectives and insights that lead to more innovative solutions. This can be facilitated through initiatives such as cross-functional teams, job rotations, and interdepartmental projects. By promoting cross-disciplinary collaboration, organizations can break down silos and foster a more integrated and creative approach to problem-solving.

Finally, fostering a culture of creativity requires a long-term commitment and continuous effort. It is not a one-time initiative but an ongoing process that involves regularly assessing and refining practices and strategies to ensure they continue to support and nurture creativity. This involves soliciting feedback from employees, staying attuned to emerging trends and best practices, and being willing to adapt and evolve as needed. By maintaining a steadfast commitment to fostering creativity, organizations can create a dynamic and innovative culture that drives long-term success.

In summary, fostering a culture of creativity involves a multifaceted approach that includes strong leadership, a conducive physical environment, diversity, continuous learning, recognition, collaboration, risk-taking, empowerment, cross-disciplinary collaboration, and a long-term commitment. By implementing these strategies, organizations can create an environment where creativity thrives, leading to more innovative solutions and sustained competitive advantage. This holistic approach ensures that creativity is not just a buzzword but an integral part of the organizational DNA, driving growth and success in an ever-changing market. To further embed creativity within the organizational fabric, it's essential to integrate creativity into the everyday processes and systems. One effective way to do this is through structured innovation programs. These programs can take various forms, such as idea competitions, hackathons, or innovation labs. Such initiatives provide a formal platform for employees to brainstorm and develop new ideas, often leading to breakthroughs that might not arise through regular work routines.

Leadership's Role in Innovation

In any organization, leadership is the keystone of innovation. The ability of leaders to inspire, guide, and support their teams in exploring new ideas and approaches determines the extent to which innovation can flourish. Effective leadership in innovation goes beyond simply endorsing new projects; it involves creating a culture where creativity is valued, risks are embraced, and continuous improvement is a shared goal.

Leaders set the vision and direction for innovation. This involves clearly articulating the importance of innovation to the organization's long-term success and embedding it into the company's mission and values. When leaders communicate a compelling vision for the future, it helps align the entire organization towards common goals and encourages employees to contribute innovative ideas that move the company closer to that vision. A well-defined vision serves as a North Star, guiding the organization through the uncertainties and complexities inherent in the innovation process.

Building a team that embodies diverse perspectives is crucial for fostering innovation. Leaders must be intentional about recruiting and retaining individuals from varied backgrounds, experiences, and skill sets. Diversity in teams leads to a richer pool of ideas and solutions, as each member brings unique insights that can challenge conventional thinking and spark creativity. By championing diversity, leaders not only enhance the potential for innovation but also create a more inclusive and dynamic workplace.

Empowering employees is another key responsibility of leaders in driving innovation. This means granting team members the autonomy to experiment, make decisions, and take ownership of their projects. When employees feel trusted and empowered, they are more likely to take initiative and explore uncharted territories. Leaders can foster this sense of empowerment by providing the necessary resources, removing bureaucratic obstacles, and encouraging a mindset that values experimentation over perfection.

Creating an environment where failure is viewed as a learning opportunity rather than a setback is essential for innovation. Leaders must exemplify this attitude by openly discussing their own failures and the lessons learned from them. By normalizing failure, leaders can reduce the fear of taking risks among employees and promote a culture where innovative ideas are pursued with enthusiasm and resilience. This approach not only cultivates a more innovative workforce but also builds a foundation of trust and psychological safety, where team members feel comfortable sharing unconventional ideas.

The role of leaders in providing continuous learning opportunities cannot be overstated. Innovation thrives in environments where employees are encouraged to expand their knowledge and skills. Leaders should invest in training programs, workshops, and other educational resources that help employees stay abreast of the latest trends and technologies. Moreover, fostering a culture of curiosity, where lifelong learning is valued, can inspire employees to seek out new information and apply it creatively to their work.

Leaders must also excel at recognizing and rewarding innovation. Acknowledging the efforts and successes of individuals and teams who contribute innovative ideas reinforces the importance of innovation within the organization. This recognition can take various forms, from formal awards and promotions to informal praise and public acknowledgment. By celebrating innovation, leaders can motivate employees to continue pushing the boundaries and striving for excellence.

Collaboration is a critical component of innovation, and leaders play a vital role in facilitating it. Encouraging cross-functional teams and providing platforms for collaboration can lead to the cross-pollination of ideas and more comprehensive solutions. Leaders should create opportunities for employees from different departments to work together, share insights, and leverage each other's expertise. This collaborative approach not only enhances innovation but also fosters a sense of unity and shared purpose within the organization.

Effective communication is another cornerstone of leadership in innovation. Leaders must be adept at conveying their vision, expectations, and feedback in a clear and inspiring manner. Transparent communication helps build trust, ensures everyone is on the same page, and reduces misunderstandings. Additionally, leaders should actively listen to their teams, valuing their input and demonstrating that their opinions matter. This two-way communication fosters a more engaged and motivated workforce, ready to contribute to the organization's innovative endeavors.

Leaders also need to be champions of change, guiding their organizations through the complexities of the innovation process. This involves being adaptable and open to new ideas, even when they challenge the status quo. Leaders must be willing to pivot strategies when necessary and embrace change as an integral part of growth. By modeling a flexible and forward-thinking attitude, leaders can inspire their teams to approach challenges with a similar mindset, fostering a culture of continuous improvement and innovation.

Mentorship and coaching are powerful tools leaders can use to nurture innovation. By providing guidance and support to employees, leaders can help them develop their creative thinking skills and navigate the challenges of bringing new ideas to fruition. Mentorship relationships can also serve as a conduit for knowledge transfer, ensuring that valuable insights and experiences are shared across the organization. Through mentorship, leaders can cultivate the next generation of innovators, ensuring the sustainability of the organization's innovative efforts.

In addition to fostering an internal culture of innovation, leaders must also be outward-looking, staying attuned to external trends and opportunities. This involves maintaining a keen awareness of industry developments, competitor activities, and emerging technologies. Leaders should encourage their teams to engage with external networks, attend industry conferences, and collaborate with external partners. By staying connected to the broader ecosystem, leaders can identify new opportunities for innovation and ensure their organizations remain at the forefront of their industries.

Ultimately, the role of leadership in innovation is multifaceted and dynamic. Leaders must be visionaries, empowering their teams, fostering a culture of learning and risk-taking, and facilitating collaboration and communication. They must also be adaptable and forward-thinking, guiding their organizations through the complexities of the innovation process. By embodying these qualities, leaders can create an environment where innovation thrives, driving long-term success and competitive advantage.

In conclusion, leadership is the driving force behind successful innovation. By setting a clear vision, empowering employees, embracing diversity, encouraging risk-taking, and fostering continuous learning and collaboration, leaders can cultivate a culture where creativity and innovation flourish. This holistic approach ensures that innovation is not just an isolated effort but a fundamental part of the organization's DNA, enabling it to adapt, grow, and succeed in an ever-changing landscape. The sustained commitment of leaders to nurturing innovation is essential for building resilient, forward-thinking organizations poised for long-term success. Leaders must also recognize the importance of fostering a supportive environment that nurtures mental and emotional well-being, as these factors significantly impact creativity and innovation. High levels of stress and burnout can stifle creative thinking and diminish employees' ability to engage in innovative activities. Leaders should prioritize creating a healthy work-life balance, offering support programs, and promoting a positive workplace culture where employees feel valued and motivated.

Encouraging Risk-Taking and Experimentation

Taking risks and experimenting with new ideas are essential for personal and professional growth. These practices foster innovation, creativity, and resilience. While the notion of risk-taking might evoke fear and uncertainty, it also opens doors to opportunities that can lead to significant breakthroughs. Encouraging yourself and others to embrace risk and experimentation involves cultivating a mindset that views failure as a learning opportunity rather than a setback.

To start, understanding the psychology behind risk-taking is crucial. Humans are naturally wired to avoid risk due to evolutionary survival instincts. However, modern society's challenges and opportunities often require us to go beyond our comfort zones. By reframing the concept of risk, we can begin to see it as a necessary step toward achieving our goals. Instead of viewing risk as a potential for loss, consider it as a chance for growth and development.

One effective way to foster a risk-taking mentality is by creating a safe environment where failure is accepted and even celebrated. This can be done in various ways, whether in a workplace, a classroom, or even within your personal life. Encouraging open communication about mistakes and what can be learned from them helps to reduce the stigma associated with failure. When people feel safe to take risks without fear of severe consequences, they are more likely to innovate and experiment.

Leaders play a pivotal role in promoting risk-taking and experimentation. By modeling these behaviors themselves, leaders can set a powerful example. When leaders take calculated risks and openly discuss their thought processes and outcomes, it demystifies the concept of risk-taking for their teams. It's important for leaders to share both their successes and failures, highlighting the lessons learned from each experience. This transparency builds trust and encourages others to follow suit.

Another key aspect of encouraging risk-taking is to provide the necessary resources and support. This includes access to information, tools, and training that can help mitigate potential risks. Providing a framework for decision-making that includes risk assessment and management strategies can empower individuals to take risks more confidently. For instance, teaching people how to analyze potential outcomes, plan for contingencies, and measure the impact of their actions can reduce the perceived threat of taking risks.

Experimentation goes hand-in-hand with risk-taking. To foster a culture of experimentation, it's important to encourage curiosity and a desire to explore new ideas. This can be achieved by dedicating time and resources to experimentation. For example, companies like Google have famously implemented the 20% time rule, where employees are encouraged to spend 20% of their time working on projects that interest them, regardless of their direct job responsibilities. This approach not only sparks creativity but also leads to innovative solutions that may not have emerged through conventional pathways.

In addition to organizational strategies, personal practices can also enhance one's ability to take risks and experiment. Developing a growth mindset, as proposed by psychologist Carol Dweck, is fundamental. A growth mindset embraces challenges, persists in the face of setbacks, and sees effort as the path to mastery. By cultivating this mindset, individuals are more likely to take risks and view failures as opportunities to learn and improve.

Mindfulness and self-awareness are also valuable tools for encouraging risk-taking. Being mindful allows individuals to recognize their fears and anxieties without being overwhelmed by them. Techniques such as meditation and reflective journaling can help in understanding the root causes of fear and developing strategies to manage them. Self-awareness enables individuals to identify their strengths and weaknesses, which can inform their risk-taking decisions and help them approach challenges with greater confidence.

Collaborative efforts can also enhance risk-taking and experimentation. Working in diverse teams brings a variety of perspectives and expertise, which can lead to more innovative solutions. Collaboration reduces the individual burden of risk, as team members can share responsibilities and support each other through the process. Encouraging cross-functional teams and interdisciplinary projects can break down silos and foster a culture where experimentation is the norm.

Feedback is another crucial element in promoting risk-taking and experimentation. Constructive feedback helps individuals understand what works and what doesn't, providing valuable insights for future attempts. It's important to create feedback mechanisms that are timely, specific, and actionable. Whether through formal review processes or informal discussions, feedback should focus on behaviors and outcomes rather than personal attributes, ensuring it is perceived as a tool for growth rather than criticism.

Balancing short-term and long-term perspectives is essential when encouraging risk-taking. While immediate results are often necessary to maintain momentum and motivation, it's equally important to keep an eye on long-term goals. This balance can be achieved by setting clear objectives and milestones that align with both short-term achievements and long-term aspirations. By doing so, individuals and organizations can take calculated risks that contribute to sustainable growth and development.

Recognizing and rewarding risk-taking and experimentation can further reinforce these behaviors. Celebrating successes, no matter how small, and acknowledging the effort put into taking risks can motivate others to follow suit. Rewards don't always have to be monetary; public recognition, opportunities for professional development, and increased autonomy can be powerful incentives. Creating a culture where risk-taking is valued and rewarded encourages continuous innovation and improvement.

Finally, storytelling can be a powerful tool in promoting risk-taking and experimentation. Sharing stories of successful risk-takers and experimenters can inspire others to take similar steps. These stories can come from within the organization or from external sources. Highlighting diverse examples, from different fields and backgrounds, can show that anyone can take risks and succeed, regardless of their starting point.

Encouraging risk-taking and experimentation is a multifaceted endeavor that requires a supportive environment, strong leadership, adequate resources, and a culture that values learning and growth. By embracing these principles, individuals and organizations can unlock their full potential, drive innovation, and achieve remarkable success. Taking risks and experimenting with new ideas may be challenging, but the rewards are well worth the effort. To further enhance the practice of risk-taking and experimentation, it is essential to integrate these principles into the fabric of daily operations and personal routines. This can be achieved through several practical strategies that ensure risk-taking and experimentation become habitual and instinctive behaviors.

Tools for Collaborative Innovation

Innovation thrives in environments where collaboration is encouraged and supported with the right tools. To harness the collective creativity and expertise of a team, it is essential to leverage tools that facilitate seamless communication, efficient project management, and robust idea generation. These tools not only streamline the collaborative process but also ensure that every team member's contributions are valued and effectively integrated into the innovation pipeline.

One of the foundational elements of collaborative innovation is effective communication. Tools like Slack, Microsoft Teams, and Zoom have revolutionized how teams interact, breaking down geographical barriers and enabling real-time collaboration. Slack, for instance, offers channels for different projects or topics, direct messaging, and integration with other productivity tools, making it a versatile platform for team communication. Microsoft Teams combines chat, video conferencing, and file sharing in one place, fostering a unified communication hub. Zoom, primarily known for its video conferencing capabilities, supports face-to-face interactions, which are crucial for brainstorming sessions and team meetings.

Beyond communication, project management tools play a critical role in organizing and tracking innovation projects. Trello, Asana, and Monday.com are among the most popular project management platforms that help teams manage tasks, deadlines, and responsibilities. Trello uses a card and board system inspired by the Kanban methodology, allowing teams to visualize project stages and progress. Asana offers more detailed task management features, enabling teams to create tasks, assign them to team members, set deadlines, and track progress through various views like lists, boards, and calendars. Monday.com provides a highly customizable interface where teams can create workflows tailored to their specific needs, making it easier to manage complex projects.

For idea generation and brainstorming, tools like Miro, MindMeister, and Stormboard are invaluable. Miro is an online collaborative whiteboard platform that allows teams to map out ideas, create diagrams, and collaborate in real-time. Its intuitive interface supports a range of activities, from simple brainstorms to complex design thinking sessions. MindMeister focuses on mind mapping, helping teams visually organize ideas and explore connections between them. This can be particularly useful during the initial stages of innovation when defining problems and identifying opportunities. Stormboard combines sticky notes and whiteboard functionalities, enabling teams to capture and organize ideas during virtual brainstorming sessions efficiently.

Document collaboration is another critical aspect of collaborative innovation. Google Workspace (formerly G Suite) and Microsoft 365 offer powerful tools for creating, sharing, and editing documents in real-time. Google Docs, Sheets, and Slides allow multiple users to work on the same document simultaneously, with changes reflected in real-time and a comprehensive version history to track edits. Microsoft 365 provides similar capabilities with Word, Excel, and PowerPoint, along with robust integration with Microsoft Teams for seamless collaboration. These tools ensure that all team members have access to the latest versions of documents and can contribute their insights and expertise.

In addition to these core tools, there are specialized platforms designed to foster innovation through collaboration. Idea management tools like IdeaScale, Brightidea, and Spigit help organizations capture, evaluate, and develop ideas from employees, customers, and other stakeholders. IdeaScale allows users to submit ideas, comment on others, and vote on the best suggestions, creating a democratic process for innovation. Brightidea offers a comprehensive suite of tools for idea collection, evaluation, and implementation, integrating with other enterprise systems to ensure seamless workflow. Spigit uses advanced algorithms to identify the most promising ideas and facilitate their development into actionable projects.

To support collaborative innovation, it is also essential to create an environment that encourages experimentation and risk-taking. Platforms like Notion and Airtable provide flexible and customizable workspaces where teams can experiment with different workflows and project management approaches. Notion combines note-taking, task management, and database functionalities in one platform, allowing teams to create tailored workspaces that suit their specific needs. Airtable offers a spreadsheet-database hybrid, enabling teams to organize and manage data in a highly customizable and visual format. These tools support agile and iterative approaches to innovation, where teams can continuously refine their processes based on feedback and evolving needs.

Effective collaboration also requires tools for feedback and evaluation. Survey tools like SurveyMonkey and Typeform enable teams to gather feedback from stakeholders, customers, and team members, providing valuable insights that can inform innovation efforts. SurveyMonkey offers a range of survey templates and advanced analytics to help teams design effective surveys and interpret results. Typeform stands out with its interactive and user-friendly interface, encouraging higher response rates and more engaging feedback experiences. Incorporating feedback mechanisms ensures that innovation efforts are aligned with the needs and preferences of stakeholders, increasing the likelihood of successful outcomes.

In the realm of collaborative innovation, it is crucial to consider the security and privacy of the tools being used. Ensuring that sensitive information and intellectual property are protected is paramount. Tools like LastPass and 1Password help teams manage passwords securely, reducing the risk of unauthorized access. Additionally, using platforms with robust encryption and compliance with industry standards, such as GDPR and HIPAA, ensures that data is handled responsibly and securely.

To maximize the effectiveness of these collaborative tools, it is important to foster a culture that values and supports collaboration. This involves setting clear expectations for communication, encouraging open and respectful dialogue, and recognizing and rewarding collaborative efforts. Leaders play a key role in modeling collaborative behaviors and providing the necessary resources and support for teams to succeed. By creating a culture that celebrates collaboration and innovation, organizations can unlock the full potential of their teams.

Ultimately, the tools for collaborative innovation are only as effective as the people using them. Investing in training and development to ensure that team members are proficient in using these tools is essential. Regularly reviewing and updating the toolset based on feedback and evolving needs ensures that teams have access to the most effective and relevant resources. By continuously refining the tools and processes for collaborative innovation, organizations can stay ahead of the curve and drive sustained success.

In conclusion, leveraging the right tools for collaborative innovation can significantly enhance a team's ability to generate, develop, and implement new ideas. From communication and project management to idea generation and feedback, these tools provide the foundation for effective collaboration. By fostering a supportive culture and investing in the necessary resources and training, organizations can create an environment where innovation thrives. Embracing collaborative innovation is not only a pathway to success but also a catalyst for continuous improvement and growth. In addition to utilizing the right tools and fostering a supportive culture, it is crucial to integrate these elements seamlessly into the organization's broader strategy. This involves ensuring that collaborative innovation is aligned with the organization's goals, values, and vision. When innovation efforts are strategically aligned, they can drive meaningful and sustainable impact.

Measuring and Rewarding Innovation within Teams

Quantifying and incentivizing innovation within teams is a nuanced and multifaceted endeavor. It demands a careful balance of metrics, recognition, and rewards that not only drive performance but also foster a culture of creativity and continuous improvement. Measuring innovation involves identifying the right indicators that reflect both the process and the outcomes of innovative efforts. Rewarding it requires understanding what motivates individuals and teams, ensuring that the recognition systems are fair, transparent, and aligned with organizational goals.

To start, it's essential to define what constitutes innovation in your organization. Innovation can take many forms, from incremental improvements to breakthrough inventions. By articulating a clear definition, you set the stage for developing meaningful metrics. For instance, innovation might be defined as the introduction of new products, services, processes, or business models that generate significant value for the organization and its customers.

Once you have a definition, the next step is to establish metrics that capture the various dimensions of innovation. These metrics should include input, process, output, and impact indicators. Input metrics might track the resources allocated to innovation activities, such as budget, time, and personnel. Process metrics could measure the efficiency and effectiveness of innovation workflows, including the number of ideas generated, the speed of prototype development, and the rate of idea implementation.

Output metrics, on the other hand, focus on the tangible results of innovation efforts. These might include the number of new products launched, patents filed, or process improvements implemented. Impact metrics go a step further, assessing the broader effects of innovation on organizational performance. These could encompass revenue growth, market share expansion, cost savings, or customer satisfaction improvements attributable to innovation.

For example, consider a company that has recently rolled out a new customer feedback system to capture insights directly from users. Input metrics might include the investment in the technology and training hours for staff. Process metrics could track the number of feedback entries received and processed each month. Output metrics might measure the number of product enhancements initiated based on this feedback. Finally, impact metrics would look at the overall increase in customer satisfaction scores and the subsequent rise in repeat purchases or referrals.

While quantitative metrics are crucial, qualitative measures also play an important role in assessing innovation. These might include peer reviews, case studies, and narrative reports that provide context and depth to the numbers. For instance, a team might submit a detailed report on a successful project, highlighting the challenges they faced, the creative solutions they developed, and the lessons learned.

With a robust measurement framework in place, the next challenge is to design a rewards system that encourages and sustains innovative behavior. Rewards can take various forms, from monetary bonuses and promotions to public recognition and opportunities for professional development. The key is to ensure that the rewards system is perceived as fair and motivating by all team members.

Monetary rewards, such as bonuses or profit-sharing, are straightforward and can be highly motivating. However, they should be carefully structured to avoid encouraging short-term thinking or unhealthy competition. For example, linking bonuses to the successful implementation of innovative projects rather than just the number of ideas generated can help focus efforts on meaningful outcomes.

Non-monetary rewards, such as recognition and professional growth opportunities, can be equally effective. Public recognition, such as awards or mentions in company communications, can boost morale and reinforce a culture of innovation. Opportunities for professional development, such as attending conferences, receiving additional training, or participating in high-visibility projects, can also be powerful motivators.

Consider a scenario where a team has successfully developed a new product feature that significantly enhances user experience. In addition to a financial bonus, the team members might be recognized at a company-wide meeting, highlighting their contributions and the positive impact of their work. Furthermore, they might be given the opportunity to present their project at an industry conference, showcasing their expertise and enhancing their professional reputation.

It's also important to recognize the role of intrinsic motivation in driving innovation. Many individuals are motivated by the inherent satisfaction of solving problems, making a positive impact, and being part of a dynamic and forward-thinking team. Creating an environment that supports autonomy, mastery, and purpose can help tap into these intrinsic motivators. For instance, giving teams the freedom to explore new ideas, providing opportunities for skill development, and aligning innovation efforts with a broader mission or vision can enhance intrinsic motivation.

To ensure that the rewards system is effective, it should be regularly reviewed and refined based on feedback from team members and the outcomes of innovation efforts. This involves soliciting input from employees about what types of rewards they find most motivating and adjusting the system accordingly. It also means monitoring the impact of rewards on innovation performance and making adjustments to address any unintended consequences.

For example, if feedback indicates that team members feel the current rewards system favors individual contributions over team efforts, adjustments might be made to better recognize collaborative achievements. Or, if data shows that monetary bonuses are leading to a focus on quantity over quality of ideas, the criteria for rewards might be revised to include qualitative assessments of innovation impact.

Finally, fostering a culture of innovation requires more than just measuring and rewarding it. It involves creating an environment where experimentation is encouraged, failures are seen as learning opportunities, and continuous improvement is valued. Leaders play a crucial role in modeling these behaviors, providing the necessary resources and support, and celebrating successes and learning experiences alike.

For instance, a leader might share stories of past failures and the valuable lessons learned from them, demonstrating that taking risks and learning from mistakes is an integral part of the innovation process. They might also ensure that teams have access to the tools, training, and resources they need to experiment and innovate effectively.

In conclusion, measuring and rewarding innovation within teams is a complex but essential task. It requires a thoughtful approach to defining innovation, developing comprehensive metrics, and designing a rewards system that motivates and sustains innovative behavior. By aligning these efforts with organizational goals, recognizing both individual and team contributions, and fostering a culture of continuous learning and improvement, organizations can drive meaningful and sustained innovation. The ultimate goal is to create an environment where creativity thrives, and innovative ideas can flourish, driving the organization forward in an ever-changing landscape. One effective strategy to sustain this environment is to embed innovation as a core value within the organizational culture. This involves not only verbal endorsements from leadership but also integrating innovation into everyday practices and decision-making processes. When innovation is deeply rooted in the company's DNA, it becomes a natural part of how work is done rather than an occasional effort.

Chapter 4

Strategic Planning for Innovation

Developing an Innovation Strategy

Crafting a robust innovation strategy is fundamental to ensuring an organization remains competitive and forward-thinking. An effective strategy not only outlines the vision for innovation but also establishes the frameworks and processes necessary to turn that vision into reality. It requires a deep understanding of the organization's goals, market dynamics, and the internal capabilities that can be leveraged. This chapter will guide you through the essential steps to develop an impactful innovation strategy.

The first step in developing an innovation strategy is to clearly define the innovation objectives. These objectives should align with the overall strategic goals of the organization. For instance, if a company's goal is to expand into new markets, the innovation strategy might focus on developing new products or services tailored to those markets. Conversely, if the goal is to improve operational efficiency, the strategy might emphasize process innovations.

To set these objectives, it is crucial to engage with key stakeholders, including senior leadership, department heads, and frontline employees. Their insights can provide a comprehensive view of the opportunities and challenges the organization faces. For example, senior leadership might highlight strategic priorities, while frontline employees can offer practical insights into areas ripe for improvement.

Once the innovation objectives are defined, the next step is to conduct a thorough analysis of the current state of innovation within the organization. This involves assessing existing processes, resources, and capabilities. A useful tool for this assessment is the innovation audit, which evaluates the organization's innovation activities, culture, and outcomes. The audit can reveal strengths to build on and gaps that need addressing.

Consider a company that discovers through its innovation audit that while it has a strong culture of idea generation, it lacks a structured process for evaluating and implementing those ideas. This insight can guide the development of a more effective innovation pipeline.

With a clear understanding of the current state, the organization can then identify the key areas where innovation will have the most impact. These areas should be prioritized based on their alignment with strategic objectives and their potential for value creation. For instance, a technology company might prioritize innovations in artificial intelligence and machine learning if these areas are critical to its competitive advantage.

After prioritizing key areas, it is essential to establish a framework for managing innovation. This framework should include processes for idea generation, evaluation, development, and implementation. A structured approach ensures that innovation efforts are systematic and aligned with organizational goals.

One effective method for managing innovation is the stage-gate process. This process divides the innovation journey into distinct stages, with specific criteria for moving from one stage to the next. For example, an idea might start with a concept development stage, followed by feasibility analysis, prototype development, and finally, market launch. At each stage, the idea is evaluated against predefined criteria to ensure it meets the necessary standards before progressing.

In addition to the stage-gate process, organizations should also foster a culture that supports innovation. This involves creating an environment where employees feel empowered to share their ideas and take risks. Leadership plays a crucial role in setting this tone. Leaders should model innovative behavior, celebrate successes, and view failures as learning opportunities rather than setbacks.

Consider the example of a company that implements regular innovation workshops where employees from different departments come together to brainstorm and develop new ideas. These workshops not only generate fresh ideas but also reinforce the value the organization places on innovation.

Another critical component of an innovation strategy is resource allocation. Innovation requires investment in terms of time, money, and talent. Organizations need to ensure they have the necessary resources to support their innovation initiatives. This might involve allocating a specific budget for innovation projects, dedicating time for employees to work on innovative ideas, or hiring new talent with the skills needed to drive innovation.

For instance, a company might set aside a portion of its annual budget specifically for funding innovation projects. This dedicated funding ensures that promising ideas have the financial support needed to be developed and implemented.

In addition to financial resources, organizations should also invest in building the skills and capabilities needed for innovation. This might involve training programs, workshops, or partnerships with external experts. For example, a company could offer design thinking workshops to help employees develop the skills needed to empathize with customers, define problems clearly, and ideate creative solutions.

Collaboration is another vital element of an effective innovation strategy. Innovation often happens at the intersection of different perspectives and expertise. Encouraging cross-functional collaboration can lead to more creative and effective solutions. Organizations should create opportunities for employees from different departments to work together on innovation projects.

Consider a healthcare company that brings together its medical professionals, IT experts, and customer service representatives to develop a new patient management system. The diverse perspectives of these team members can lead to a more comprehensive and user-friendly solution.

In addition to internal collaboration, organizations should also look for opportunities to collaborate with external partners. This might include partnerships with other companies, research institutions, or startups. External collaborations can provide access to new ideas, technologies, and markets.

For example, a consumer goods company might partner with a tech startup to develop smart packaging solutions. This partnership can combine the consumer goods company's market knowledge with the startup's technological expertise to create innovative products.

Once the innovation strategy is in place, it is essential to establish metrics to measure progress and impact. These metrics should be aligned with the innovation objectives and provide a clear picture of how well the strategy is working. Common innovation metrics include the number of new products launched, revenue generated from new products, and the time it takes to bring an idea to market.

For instance, a company might track the percentage of total revenue generated from products launched in the past three years. This metric provides insight into the impact of innovation on the company's growth.

Regularly reviewing and refining the innovation strategy is also crucial. The business environment is constantly changing, and the innovation strategy should be flexible enough to adapt to new opportunities and challenges. Organizations should establish a process for regularly reviewing their innovation strategy and making adjustments as needed.

Consider a company that conducts quarterly reviews of its innovation strategy. During these reviews, the company assesses its progress against the defined objectives, evaluates the impact of its innovation initiatives, and identifies any necessary adjustments. This iterative approach ensures that the innovation strategy remains relevant and effective.

In conclusion, developing an innovation strategy involves a systematic approach to defining objectives, assessing the current state, prioritizing key areas, establishing a management framework, allocating resources, fostering a supportive culture, encouraging collaboration, and measuring progress. By following these steps, organizations can create a comprehensive and flexible innovation strategy that drives sustained success and growth. An effective innovation strategy also hinges on the ability to dynamically pivot when necessary. This adaptability is crucial in today's fast-paced business environment, where market conditions, customer preferences, and technological advancements can shift rapidly. Organizations that can quickly respond to these changes are better positioned to capitalize on new opportunities and mitigate potential risks.

Aligning Innovation with Business Goals

Moreover, leadership plays an instrumental role in sustaining this alignment. Effective leaders are not only visionaries but also enablers who remove barriers to innovation and cultivate an environment where new ideas can flourish. They must be adept at balancing the need for short-term results with long-term innovation goals, ensuring that the organization does not become overly focused on immediate gains at the expense of future growth.

A key responsibility of leadership in this context is to foster open communication and transparency. Employees at all levels should feel empowered to share their ideas and feedback without fear of retribution. This open dialogue can uncover valuable insights and spur innovation that might otherwise remain untapped. Leaders should actively seek input from diverse teams and create forums where employees can voice their thoughts on strategic priorities and innovation initiatives. Moreover, leadership plays an instrumental role in sustaining this alignment. Effective leaders are not only visionaries but also enablers who remove barriers to innovation and cultivate an environment where new ideas can flourish. They must be adept at balancing the need for short-term results with long-term innovation goals, ensuring that the organization does not become overly focused on immediate gains at the expense of future growth.

Resource Allocation for Innovation Projects

Resource allocation for innovation projects is a critical aspect that can make or break an organization's pursuit of new ideas and technologies. Ensuring that resources—whether financial, human, or technological—are effectively allocated requires a strategic approach that aligns with the company's overall objectives and maximizes the potential for successful outcomes.

Understanding the types of resources required for innovation is the first step. Financial resources are often the most visible and include budgets for research and development, prototyping, testing, and market introduction. Human resources encompass the talent and expertise needed to drive innovation, from creative thinkers and engineers to project managers and marketing specialists. Technological resources involve the tools, software, and infrastructure necessary to support innovative activities.

To allocate these resources effectively, organizations must begin with a clear understanding of their strategic priorities. This involves identifying key areas where innovation can significantly impact the business, such as product development, process improvement, or market expansion. By aligning resource allocation with these priorities, companies can ensure that their investments in innovation are directed towards initiatives that offer the highest potential returns.

One effective method for prioritizing innovation projects is the use of a project portfolio management approach. This involves evaluating each potential project based on criteria such as strategic alignment, potential impact, feasibility, and risk. Projects that score highest on these criteria are prioritized for resource allocation. This structured approach helps organizations avoid the pitfalls of spreading resources too thinly across too many projects, which can dilute the effectiveness of their innovation efforts.

Consider the example of a pharmaceutical company that uses a project portfolio management approach to allocate resources for drug development. The company evaluates each potential project based on factors such as the unmet medical need it addresses, the potential market size, and the probability of regulatory approval. By focusing resources on the most promising projects, the company increases its chances of bringing successful products to market.

Another crucial aspect of resource allocation is ensuring that the right talent is assigned to innovation projects. This involves identifying individuals with the necessary skills and expertise and creating cross-functional teams that can collaborate effectively. Innovation often requires a diverse set of perspectives, so assembling teams with varied backgrounds and areas of expertise can lead to more creative solutions.

For example, a technology company might assemble a team for a new product development project that includes software developers, hardware engineers, user experience designers, and marketing professionals. By bringing together individuals with different skill sets, the company can ensure that all aspects of the product are considered, from technical feasibility to user experience and market appeal.

In addition to assembling the right teams, organizations must also invest in training and development to ensure that their employees have the skills needed to drive innovation. This includes not only technical skills but also soft skills such as creative thinking, problem-solving, and collaboration. Providing opportunities for continuous learning and professional development can help employees stay abreast of emerging trends and technologies, enabling them to contribute more effectively to innovation projects.

For instance, a manufacturing company might offer regular workshops and training sessions on topics such as lean manufacturing, data analytics, and sustainability. These programs can help employees develop the skills needed to identify and implement innovative solutions that improve operational efficiency and reduce environmental impact.

Effective resource allocation also involves creating a supportive environment that encourages innovation. This includes providing the necessary tools and infrastructure, such as state-of-the-art laboratories, prototyping equipment, and collaborative workspaces. It also involves fostering a culture that supports risk-taking and experimentation, recognizing that not all innovation projects will succeed but that each failure provides valuable learning opportunities.

Leadership plays a critical role in creating this supportive environment. Leaders must communicate the importance of innovation and demonstrate their commitment through actions and decisions. This might involve setting aside dedicated time for employees to work on innovative projects, providing seed funding for promising ideas, or recognizing and rewarding innovative contributions.

Consider a scenario in which a company's leadership team allocates a portion of the annual budget specifically for innovation grants. Employees can apply for these grants to fund pilot projects or explore new ideas. This not only provides the financial resources needed for innovation but also signals to employees that the company values and supports their creative efforts.

In addition to financial and human resources, technological resources are essential for supporting innovation. This includes investing in the latest tools and technologies that can facilitate innovative activities, such as advanced software for data analysis, simulation tools for prototyping, and collaboration platforms that enable remote teamwork. Staying current with technological advancements can provide organizations with a competitive edge and enhance their ability to innovate.

For instance, a financial services company might invest in advanced data analytics software to identify trends and insights that can inform the development of new financial products. By leveraging cutting-edge technology, the company can gain a deeper understanding of customer needs and market dynamics, enabling it to innovate more effectively.

Another important consideration in resource allocation is the need for flexibility. Innovation is inherently uncertain, and projects may need to pivot or adjust course as new information becomes available. Organizations must be willing to reallocate resources as needed, whether that means increasing funding for a project that shows promise or redirecting resources from a project that is not meeting expectations.

For example, a consumer goods company might start an innovation project to develop a new eco-friendly packaging solution. During the project, the team discovers a more cost-effective and sustainable material than initially anticipated. Recognizing the potential of this new material, the company decides to reallocate additional resources to accelerate its development and bring the solution to market faster.

Finally, monitoring and evaluating the impact of resource allocation decisions is essential for continuous improvement. Organizations should establish metrics and key performance indicators (KPIs) to track the progress and outcomes of innovation projects. Regular reviews of these metrics can provide insights into the effectiveness of resource allocation and inform future decisions.

Common KPIs for innovation projects include the number of new products launched, the revenue generated from new products, the time-to-market for innovation initiatives, and customer satisfaction with new offerings. By regularly reviewing these metrics, organizations can assess the success of their innovation efforts and make data-driven adjustments to their resource allocation strategies.

For instance, a healthcare organization might track the number of new medical devices brought to market and the revenue generated from these devices. If the metrics indicate that certain projects are consistently outperforming others, the organization can analyze the factors contributing to their success and apply these insights to future resource allocation decisions.

In conclusion, effective resource allocation for innovation projects requires a strategic approach that aligns with organizational priorities, assembles the right talent, invests in training and development, creates a supportive environment, leverages technological advancements, maintains flexibility, and continuously monitors and evaluates progress. By carefully managing resources and fostering a culture that supports innovation, organizations can maximize the potential for successful outcomes and drive long-term growth and competitiveness. Moreover, organizations should consider the importance of fostering external partnerships and collaborations as part of their resource allocation strategy. Collaborating with external entities such as universities, research institutions, startups, and other corporations can provide access to additional resources, knowledge, and technologies that may not be available internally. These partnerships can accelerate innovation by bringing in fresh perspectives, specialized expertise, and novel technologies.

Risk Management in Innovation Planning

Risk management in innovation planning is a crucial yet often underappreciated component of successful innovation strategies. When embarking on innovative ventures, the inherent uncertainty and potential for failure can be daunting. However, with a structured approach to identifying, assessing, and mitigating risks, organizations can better navigate these uncertainties and increase their chances of achieving breakthrough success.

The first step in effective risk management is recognizing the types of risks that can impact innovation projects. These risks can be broadly categorized into technical, market, financial, operational, and strategic risks. Technical risks pertain to the feasibility and functionality of the technology or product being developed. Market risks involve the potential for market acceptance and the competitive landscape. Financial risks concern the availability of funds and the potential for cost overruns. Operational risks relate to the execution of the project, including resource allocation and timeline adherence. Strategic risks involve the alignment of the innovation project with the organization's long-term goals and the potential for changes in the business environment.

To illustrate, consider a company developing a new type of wearable health monitor. Technical risks might include the challenge of miniaturizing sensors without losing accuracy. Market risks could involve uncertainty about whether consumers will adopt the new device in a crowded market. Financial risks might arise from the high costs of research and development. Operational risks could include delays in the supply chain for critical components. Strategic risks might involve a shift in regulatory requirements for health monitoring devices.

Once these risks are identified, the next step is to assess their potential impact and likelihood. This assessment helps prioritize which risks need more immediate and intensive management efforts. A common approach is to use a risk matrix, which plots the likelihood of each risk occurring against its potential impact. Risks that are both highly likely and have significant impacts are prioritized for mitigation.

For example, in the case of the wearable health monitor, if the technical risk of sensor miniaturization is both highly likely to occur and would have a significant impact on the project's success, it would be prioritized for mitigation efforts. Conversely, if market risks are deemed less likely but still potentially impactful, they would be monitored but might not require immediate action.

Mitigation strategies are then developed for the prioritized risks. These strategies can include avoidance, reduction, transfer, or acceptance. Avoidance involves changing the project plan to eliminate the risk, reduction involves taking steps to minimize the impact or likelihood of the risk, transfer involves shifting the risk to another party (such as through insurance or outsourcing), and acceptance involves acknowledging the risk and preparing to manage its consequences if it occurs.

For instance, to mitigate the technical risk of sensor miniaturization, the company might invest in additional R&D to explore alternative technologies or partner with a specialist firm that has expertise in miniaturization. To address market risks, the company could conduct comprehensive market research to better understand consumer needs and preferences, thus reducing uncertainty about market acceptance. Financial risks might be mitigated by securing additional funding or creating a more flexible budget that can accommodate potential cost overruns. Operational risks could be mitigated by developing robust project management practices and contingency plans. Strategic risks might be addressed by regularly reviewing the project's alignment with the company's long-term goals and adjusting the project plan as necessary.

Communication plays a critical role in effective risk management. All stakeholders, including project team members, executives, and external partners, need to be informed about the identified risks and the strategies for mitigating them. Regular updates and transparent reporting help ensure that everyone is aware of the current risk landscape and any changes that might affect the project. This collaborative approach can also foster a culture of proactive risk management, where potential issues are identified and addressed early.

For example, in the wearable health monitor project, regular meetings with the project team and key stakeholders could be held to discuss the status of identified risks and the effectiveness of mitigation strategies. This open communication ensures that everyone is on the same page and can contribute to risk management efforts.

Adaptive project management techniques, such as agile methodologies, can also enhance risk management in innovation planning. Agile methodologies emphasize iterative development, frequent reassessment, and flexibility. By breaking the project into smaller, manageable components and regularly reviewing progress, organizations can quickly identify and respond to emerging risks. This approach allows for adjustments to be made in real-time, reducing the likelihood of major setbacks.

Consider a software development company using agile methodologies to develop a new application. By working in sprints and holding regular review meetings, the project team can quickly identify technical issues or user feedback that indicate potential risks. This iterative process allows the team to address these risks promptly, whether it involves tweaking the application's features or reallocating resources to areas that need more attention.

Scenario planning is another valuable tool in risk management for innovation planning. This involves envisioning different future scenarios that could impact the project and developing strategies for each scenario. By preparing for various potential outcomes, organizations can be more resilient and better equipped to handle unexpected challenges.

For example, a renewable energy company might develop scenarios for different regulatory environments, market conditions, and technological advancements. By considering how each scenario could impact their innovation projects, the company can develop contingency plans and ensure they are prepared for various possibilities.

Regularly reviewing and updating the risk management plan is essential for maintaining its effectiveness. As the project progresses and new information becomes available, the risk landscape can change. Regular reviews allow organizations to reassess risks, evaluate the effectiveness of mitigation strategies, and make necessary adjustments.

For instance, during the development of the wearable health monitor, regular risk reviews might reveal that some technical challenges have been resolved, while new market risks have emerged due to changes in consumer behavior or competitor actions. By continuously updating the risk management plan, the company can stay ahead of potential issues and maintain momentum towards successful project completion.

Leadership commitment is crucial for effective risk management in innovation planning. Leaders need to champion risk management efforts, allocate the necessary resources, and create an environment where risk management is viewed as a vital component of project success. By demonstrating their commitment, leaders can motivate the entire organization to prioritize risk management and contribute to a culture of proactive risk mitigation.

For example, if the CEO of the company developing the wearable health monitor regularly emphasizes the importance of risk management in communications with employees and stakeholders, it reinforces the message that managing risks is essential for the project's success. This top-down commitment can help ensure that risk management is integrated into every aspect of the project.

In conclusion, risk management in innovation planning is a multifaceted process that involves identifying, assessing, and mitigating various types of risks. By prioritizing risks based on their impact and likelihood, developing robust mitigation strategies, fostering open communication, and regularly reviewing and updating the risk management plan, organizations can enhance their ability to navigate uncertainties and achieve successful innovation outcomes. Adaptive project management techniques, scenario planning, and strong leadership commitment further support effective risk management, ensuring that innovation projects are resilient and well-positioned for success. Through these comprehensive risk management practices, organizations can confidently pursue innovative ventures and drive long-term growth and competitiveness. Risk management should also extend beyond the confines of individual projects to encompass a broader organizational perspective. This holistic approach ensures that the cumulative risks from multiple innovation projects are understood and managed in a coherent manner. Portfolio management techniques can be particularly useful in this context, providing a framework for balancing risks and rewards across a range of projects.

Monitoring and Adjusting Your Innovation Strategy

Success in innovation is not a one-time event but a continuous process that requires vigilant monitoring and timely adjustments. An innovation strategy, no matter how well-conceived, needs to be adaptable to the dynamic nature of markets, technologies, and consumer behaviors. The ability to monitor progress and make necessary adjustments can mean the difference between groundbreaking success and costly failure.

The initial step in monitoring an innovation strategy involves setting clear, measurable objectives. These objectives should align with the broader goals of the organization and provide specific benchmarks for success. Establishing key performance indicators (KPIs) is essential. KPIs might include metrics such as time-to-market, return on investment, customer satisfaction, and adoption rates. These indicators provide a quantitative basis for assessing progress and identifying areas that require attention.

Once objectives and KPIs are in place, collecting and analyzing data becomes crucial. Data can be gathered from various sources, including market research, customer feedback, sales figures, and internal performance metrics. Regularly reviewing this data helps organizations stay informed about the effectiveness of their innovation efforts. For instance, if a tech company launches a new software product, analyzing user engagement metrics and customer feedback can reveal whether the product meets market needs and where improvements are needed.

Consider the example of a startup developing a new mobile application for health tracking. Initially, they set objectives such as achieving 100,000 downloads within the first six months and maintaining a user retention rate of 50% after three months. To monitor these objectives, they track KPIs like daily active users, user feedback ratings, and feature usage statistics. This data provides insights into how well the app is performing and whether it is meeting user expectations.

However, data collection alone is not sufficient. The real value lies in interpreting this data to make informed decisions. This involves identifying trends, patterns, and anomalies that can indicate potential issues or opportunities. For example, if the health tracking app sees a sudden drop in user engagement, it prompts an investigation into the cause. It could be due to a recent update that introduced bugs or a competitor launching a similar product. Understanding the reasons behind the data helps in making precise adjustments to the strategy.

Regular reviews and progress meetings are vital for keeping the innovation strategy on track. These reviews should involve key stakeholders, including project managers, team members, and executives. Discussing the current status, successes, and challenges ensures that everyone is aligned and aware of any necessary adjustments. For instance, in a quarterly review meeting of the health tracking app team, they might discover that users are requesting a feature for integrating with wearable devices. Addressing this feedback quickly can enhance user satisfaction and retention.

Flexibility and agility are essential qualities in innovation management. The ability to pivot or tweak the strategy in response to new information or changing circumstances is crucial. This does not mean abandoning the original plan at the first sign of trouble but rather being open to iterative improvements. Agile methodologies, which emphasize incremental progress and continuous feedback, can be particularly effective in this regard. By breaking down the innovation process into smaller, manageable sprints, teams can frequently assess progress and make necessary adjustments.

Consider the case of an established manufacturing company venturing into smart home devices. They initially planned to develop a smart thermostat with advanced learning capabilities. Early user testing, however, revealed that potential customers found the interface too complex. Instead of scrapping the whole project, the team decided to simplify the user interface and add a guided setup feature. This adjustment, based on early feedback, significantly improved user acceptance and satisfaction.

Scenario planning is another valuable tool for monitoring and adjusting an innovation strategy. By envisioning different future scenarios, organizations can prepare for various contingencies and reduce the element of surprise. Scenario planning involves asking "what if" questions and developing strategies for each potential outcome. For example, the manufacturing company might consider scenarios where a new regulatory standard for smart devices is introduced or where a major competitor launches a similar product. By having predefined responses to these scenarios, the company can quickly adapt without significant disruption.

In addition to internal monitoring, keeping an eye on external factors is equally important. This includes staying informed about industry trends, technological advancements, and competitor activities. Market intelligence can provide early warnings about shifts that might impact the innovation strategy. For instance, if a competitor releases a groundbreaking feature in their smart thermostat, the manufacturing company needs to assess how this affects their market position and whether they need to accelerate their own feature development.

External partnerships and collaborations can also play a role in monitoring and adjusting an innovation strategy. Engaging with industry experts, research institutions, and other companies can provide fresh perspectives and insights. These collaborations can offer access to additional data, technologies, and resources that might not be available internally. For example, the manufacturing company might partner with a university research lab specializing in artificial intelligence to enhance the learning capabilities of their smart thermostat. This partnership not only brings in cutting-edge technology but also provides a broader view of potential future developments.

Leadership involvement is crucial for the effective monitoring and adjustment of an innovation strategy. Leaders need to foster a culture that values continuous improvement and is open to change. They should encourage experimentation and not penalize failure, as long as it leads to valuable lessons. By setting the tone from the top, leaders can ensure that the entire organization is committed to the ongoing process of innovation.

For instance, the CEO of the manufacturing company might hold regular innovation town halls where team members can share their progress, challenges, and ideas. This open forum encourages transparency and collaboration, ensuring that everyone feels invested in the innovation journey. It also allows leaders to stay connected with the ground realities and make informed decisions about strategic adjustments.

Finally, it is essential to celebrate successes and learn from setbacks. Recognizing and rewarding achievements boosts morale and reinforces the importance of innovation. At the same time, analyzing setbacks without assigning blame helps the organization understand what went wrong and how to avoid similar issues in the future. For example, if the smart thermostat project encounters a delay due to supply chain issues, conducting a post-mortem analysis can identify the root cause and lead to better risk management practices for future projects.

In summary, monitoring and adjusting an innovation strategy is a dynamic and ongoing process that involves setting clear objectives, collecting and analyzing data, interpreting results, conducting regular reviews, and being flexible and responsive to change. By fostering a culture of continuous improvement, leveraging scenario planning, staying informed about external factors, and promoting leadership involvement, organizations can navigate the complexities of innovation with confidence. Through diligent monitoring and timely adjustments, they can ensure that their innovation efforts remain aligned with their strategic goals and are poised for long-term success.